T0063018

Feast, Famine & Potluck

Published in South Africa by Short Story Day Africa in 2013
Registered NPO 123-206
http://shortstorydayafrica.org

Print Edition published by Hands-On Books, an imprint of Modjaji Books
PO Box 385, Athlone, 7760, Cape Town, South Africa
www.modjajibooks.co.za/titles/books/hands-on/

Print ISBN: 978-0-620-58887-4
E-book ISBN: 978-0-620-58886-7

Edited by Karen Jennings
Typesetting and cover design by Nick Mulgrew
Cover illustration by Candace di Talamo

This book was typeset in Minion Pro and Bodoni

FEAST, FAMINE & POTLUCK

SHORT STORY DAY AFRICA

INTRODUCTION   6

INTRODUCTION

In 2011, when we founded a Short Story Day in Africa, we set out a number of goals we hoped to accomplish one day. I'm proud of how many of those goals have been realised in three short years – one operating in southern Africa and two throughout Africa. This anthology of nineteen stories, collected from African writers, both established and emerging, is the pinnacle of those goals. Contained within these pages are the nineteen stories that were longlisted for Short Story Day Africa's Feast, Famine and Potluck competition.

We tailored our submissions guidelines and judging process for the competition according to needs we identified within the Short Story Africa community in 2012. Three main issues arose:

1. The desire for a platform for emerging writers to showcase their work (due to a lack of resources, we are only able to showcase the work of previously published writers on our website).
2. A sense that many African short story competitions were unfairly weighted in favour of Eurocentric writing.
3. Exclusions from competitions for various writers. i.e. What makes writing African?

We therefore decided to open the competition to any African citizen, or person who is part of the African diaspora, as well as to persons residing permanently in an African country, whether they had a publication history or not.

We received sixty-eight stories. Each story was then formatted to a standard and stripped of any identifying details, after which it was sent to two readers. The readers were asked to mark the stories out of ten, following a broad set of guidelines, but also going on gut feel — an important tool in pinpointing great art. An interesting trend emerged. The highest scoring stories were awarded equal scores by both readers or were, at most, a point apart.

The judging panel consisted of three judges, Isabella Morris, Novuyo Rosa-Tshuma and Conseulo Roland, who compiled a short list of six. These six were sent to Petina Gappah who was tasked with selecting the three overall winners. As with the reading process, all judging was blind.

The winning stories are:

1st Place: My Father's Head by Okwiri Oduor (Kenya)
2nd Place: Choke by Jayne Bauling (South Africa)
3rd Place: Chicken by Efemia Chela (Ghana)

This year, we applied for, and received, NPO status. As a Non Profit Organisation, we will be able to apply for funding, though the spirit of collaboration that has driven this project from its inception will always be at the heart of Short Story Day Africa. This project and the *Feast, Famine and Potluck* anthology would not have been possible without the overwhelming support of the African writing community and those beyond our continent's border who value the ideal set out by the Short Story Day Africa project: that Africa gets to tell its own stories, in its own voices.

I look forward to the anthology becoming a feature on the African publishing calendar in years to come.

Rachel Zadok
Founder and Short Story Day Africa Project Coordinator

– SHORTLISTED FOR THE 2014 CAINE PRIZE –

My Father's Head

Okwiri Oduor

I had meant to summon my father only long enough to see what his head looked like, but now he was here and I did not know how to send him back.

It all started the Thursday that Father Ignatius came from Immaculate Conception in Kitgum. The old women wore their Sunday frocks, and the old men plucked garlands of bougainvillea from the fence and stuck them in their breast pockets. One old man would not leave the dormitory because he could not find his shikwarusi, and when I coaxed and badgered, he patted his hair and said, "My God, do you want the priest from Uganda to think that I look like this every day?"

I arranged chairs beneath the avocado tree in the front yard, and the old people sat down and practiced their smiles. A few people who did not live at the home came too, like the woman who hawked candy in the Stagecoach bus to Mathari North, and the man whose one-roomed house was a kindergarten in the daytime and a brothel in the evening, and the woman whose illicit brew had blinded five people in January.

Father Ignatius came riding on the back of a bodaboda, and after everyone had dropped a coin in his hat, he gave the bodaboda man fifty shillings and the bodaboda man said, "Praise God," and then rode back the way he had come.

Father Ignatius took off his coat and sat down in the chair that was marked, "Father Ignatius Okello, New Chaplain," and the old people gave him the smiles they had been practicing, smiles that melted like ghee, that oozed through the corners of their lips and dribbled onto their laps long after the thing that was being smiled about went rancid in the air.

Father Ignatius said, "The Lord be with you," and the people said, "And also with you," and then they prayed and they sang and they had a feast; dipping bread slices in tea, and when the drops fell on the cuffs of their woollen sweaters, sucking at them with their steamy, cinnamon tongues.

Father Ignatius' maiden sermon was about love: love your neighbour as you love yourself, that kind of self-deprecating thing. The old people had little use for love, and although they gave Father Ignatius an ingratiating smile, what they really wanted to know was what type of place Kitgum was, and if it was true that the Bagisu people were savage cannibals.

What I wanted to know was what type of person Father Ignatius thought he was, instructing others to distribute their love like this or like that, as though one could measure love on weights, pack it inside glass jars and place it on shelves for the neighbours to pick as they pleased. As though one could look at it and say, "Now see: I have ten loves in total. Let me save three for my country and give all the rest to my neighbours."

It must have been the way that Father Ignatius filled his mug – until the tea ran over the clay rim and down the stool leg and soaked into his canvas shoe – that got me thinking about my own father. One moment I was listening to tales of Acholi valour, and the next, I was stringing together images of my father, making his limbs move and his lips spew words, so that in the end, he was a marionette and my memories of him were only scenes in a theatrical display.

Even as I showed Father Ignatius to his chambers, cleared the table, put the chairs back inside, took my purse, and dragged myself to Odeon to get a matatu to Uthiru, I thought about the millet-coloured freckle in my father's eye, and the fifty cent coins he always forgot in his coat pockets, and the way each Saturday morning men knocked on our front door and said things like, "Johnson, you have to come now; the water pipe has burst and we are filling our glasses with shit," and, "Johnson, there is no time to put on clothes even; just come the way you are. The maid gave birth in the night and flushed the baby down the toilet."

Every day after work, I bought an ear of street-roasted maize and chewed it one kernel at a time, and when I reached the house, I wiggled out of the muslin dress and wore dungarees and drank a cup of masala chai. Then I carried my father's toolbox to the bathroom. I chiselled out old broken tiles from the wall, and they fell onto my boots, and the dust rose from them and exploded in the flaring tongues of fire lapping through chinks in the stained glass.

This time, as I did all those things, I thought of the day I sat at my father's feet and he scooped a handful of groundnuts and rubbed them between his palms, chewed them, and then fed the mush to me. I was of a curious age then;

old enough to chew with my own teeth, yet young enough to desire that hot, masticated love, love that did not need to be doctrinated or measured in cough syrup caps.

The Thursday Father Ignatius came from Kitgum, I spent the entire night on my stomach on the sitting room floor, drawing my father. In my mind I could see his face, see the lines around his mouth, the tiny blobs of light in his irises, the crease at the part where his ear joined his temple. I could even see the thick line of sweat and oil on his shirt collar, the little brown veins that broke off from the main stream of dirt and ran down on their own.

I could see all these things, yet no matter what I did, his head refused to appear within the borders of the paper. I started off with his feet and worked my way up and in the end my father's head popped out of the edges of the paper and onto scuffed linoleum and plastic magnolias and the wet soles of bathroom slippers.

I showed Bwibo some of the drawings. Bwibo was the cook at the old people's home, with whom I had formed an easy camaraderie.

"My God!" Bwibo muttered, flipping through them. "Simbi, this is abnormal."

The word 'abnormal' came out crumbly, and it broke over the sharp edge of the table and became clods of loam on the plastic floor covering. Bwibo rested her head on her palm, and the bell sleeves of her cream-coloured caftan swelled as though there were pumpkins stacked inside them.

I told her what I had started to believe, that perhaps my father had had a face but no head at all. And even if my father had had a head, I would not have seen it: people's heads were not a thing that one often saw. One looked at a person, and what one saw was their face: a regular face-shaped face, that shrouded a regular head-shaped head. If the face was remarkable, one looked twice. But what was there to draw one's eyes to the banalities of another's head? Most times when one looked at a person, one did not even see their head there at all.

Bwibo stood over the waist-high jiko, poured cassava flour into a pot of bubbling water and stirred it with a cooking oar. "Child," she said, "how do you know that the man in those drawings is your father? He has no head at all, no face."

"I recognize his clothes. The red corduroys that he always paired with yellow shirts."

Bwibo shook her head. "It is only with a light basket that someone can escape the rain."

It was that time of day when the old people fondled their wooden beads and snorted off to sleep in between incantations. I allowed them a brief, bashful siesta, long enough for them to believe that they had recited the entire rosary. Then I tugged at the ropes and the lunch bells chimed. The old people sat eight to a table, and with their mouths filled with ugali, sour lentils and okra soup, said things like, "Do not buy chapati from Kadima's Kiosk— Kadima's wife sits on the dough and charms it with her buttocks," or, "Did I tell you about Wambua, the one whose cow chewed a child because the child would not stop wailing?"

In the afternoon, I emptied the bedpans and soaked the old people's feet in warm water and baking soda, and when they trooped off to mass I took my purse and went home.

The Christmas before the cane tractor killed my father, he drank his tea from plates and fried his eggs on the lids of coffee jars, and he retrieved his Yamaha drum-set from a shadowy, lizardy place in the back of the house and sat on the veranda and smoked and beat the drums until his knuckles bled.

One day he took his stool and hand-held radio and went to the veranda, and I sat at his feet, undid his laces and peeled off his gummy socks. He wiggled his toes about. They smelt slightly fetid, like sour cream.

My father smoked and listened to narrations of famine undulating deeper into the Horn of Africa, and when the clock chimed eight o'clock, he turned the knob and listened to the death news. It was not long before his ears caught the name of someone he knew. He choked on the smoke trapped in his throat.

My father said, "Did you hear that? Sospeter has gone! Sospeter, the son of Milkah, who taught Agriculture in Mirere Secondary. My God, I am telling you, everyone is going. Even me, you shall hear me on the death news very soon."

I brought him his evening cup of tea. He smashed his cigarette against the veranda, then he slowly brought the cup to his lips. The cup was filled just the way he liked it, filled until the slightest trembling would have his fingers and thighs scalded.

My father took a sip of his tea and said, "Sospeter was like a brother to me. Why did I have to learn of his death like this, over the radio?"

Later, my father lay on the fold-away sofa, and I sat on the stool watching him, afraid that if I looked away, he would go too. It was the first time I imagined his death, the first time I mourned.

And yet it was not my father I was mourning. I was mourning the image of myself inside the impossible aura of my father's death. I was imagining what it all would be like: the death news would say that my father had drowned in a cess pit, and people would stare at me as though I were a monitor lizard trapped inside a manhole in the street. I imagined that I would be wearing my green dress when I got the news – the one with red gardenias embroidered in its bodice –and people would come and pat my shoulder and give me warm Coca Cola in plastic cups and say, "I put my sorrow in a basket and brought it here as soon as I heard. How else would your father's spirit know that I am innocent of his death?"

Bwibo had an explanation as to why I could not remember the shape of my father's head.

She said, "Although everyone has a head behind their face, some show theirs easily; they turn their back on you and their head is all you can see. Your father was a good man and good men never show you their heads; they show you their faces."

Perhaps she was right. Even the day my father's people telephoned to say that a cane tractor had flattened him on the road to Shibale, no one said a thing about having seen his head. They described the rest of his body with a measured delicacy: how his legs were strewn across the road, sticky and shiny with fresh tar, and how one foot remained inside his tyre sandal, pounding the pedal of his bicycle, and how cane juice filled his mouth and soaked the collar of his polyester shirt, and how his face had a patient serenity, even as his eyes burst and rolled in the rain puddles.

And instead of weeping right away when they said all those things to me, I had wondered if my father really had come from a long line of obawami, and if his people would bury him seated in his grave, with a string of royal cowries round his neck.

"In any case," Bwibo went on, "what more is there to think about your father, eh? That milk spilled a long time ago, and it has curdled on the ground."

I spent the day in the dormitories, stripping beds, sunning mattresses, scrubbing PVC mattress pads. One of the old men kept me company. He told me how he came to spend his sunset years at the home – in August of 1998 he was at the station waiting to board the evening train back home to Mombasa. When the bomb went off at the American Embassy, the police trawled the city and arrested every man of Arab extraction. Because he was seventy-two and already rapidly unravelling into senility, they dumped him at the old people's home, and he had been there ever since.

"Did your people not come to claim you?" I asked, bewildered.

The old man snorted. "My people?"

"Everyone has people that belong to them."

The old man laughed. "Only the food you have already eaten belongs to you."

Later, the old people sat in drooping clumps in the yard. Bwibo and I watched from the back steps of the kitchen. In the grass, ants devoured a squirming caterpillar. The dog's nose, a translucent pink doodled with green veins, twitched. Birds raced each other over the frangipani. One tripped over the power line and smashed its head on the moss–covered electricity pole.

Wasps flew low over the grass. A lizard crawled over the lichen that choked a pile of timber. The dog licked the inside of its arm. A troupe of royal butterfly dancers flitted over the row of lilies, their colourful gauze dancing skirts trembling to the rumble of an inaudible drum beat. The dog lay on its side in the grass, smothering the squirming caterpillar and the chewing ants. The dog's nipples were little pellets of goat shit stuck with spit onto its furry underside.

Bwibo said, "I can help you remember the shape of your father's head."

I said, "Now what type of mud is this you have started speaking?"

Bwibo licked her index finger and held it solemnly in the air. "I swear, Bible red! I can help you and I can help you."

Let me tell you: one day you will renounce your exile, and you will go back home, and your mother will take out the finest china, and your father will slaughter a sprightly cockerel for you, and the neighbours will bring some potluck, and your sister will wear her navy blue PE wrapper, and your brother will eat with a spoon instead of squelching rice and soup through the spaces between his fingers.

And you, you will have to tell them stories about places not-here, about people that soaked their table napkins in Jik Bleach and talked about London as though London was a place one could reach by hopping onto an Akamba bus and driving by Nakuru and Kisumu and Kakamega and finding themselves there.

You will tell your people about men that did not slit melons up into slices but split them into halves and ate each of the halves out with a spoon, about women that held each other's hands around street lamps in town and skipped about, showing snippets of grey Mother's Union bloomers as they sang:

Kijembe ni kikali, param-param

Kilikata mwalimu, param-param

You think that your people belong to you, that they will always have a place for you in their minds and their hearts. You think that your people will always look forward to your return.

Maybe the day you go back home to your people you will have to sit in a wicker chair on the veranda and smoke alone because, although they may have wanted to have you back, no one really meant for you to stay.

My father was slung over the wicker chair in the veranda, just like in the old days, smoking and watching the handheld radio. The death news rose from the radio, and it became a mist, hovering low, clinging to the cold glass of the sitting room window.

My father's shirt flapped in the wind, and tendrils of smoke snapped before his face. He whistled to himself. At first the tune was a faceless, pitiful thing, like an old bottle that someone found on the path and kicked all the way home. Then the tune caught fragments of other tunes inside it, and it lost its free-spirited falling and rising.

My father had a head. I could see it now that I had the mind to look for it. His head was shaped like a butternut squash. Perhaps that was the reason I had forgotten all about it; it was a horrible, disconcerting thing to look at.

My father had been a plumber. His fingernails were still rimmed with dregs from the drainage pipes he tinkered about in, and his boots still squished with ugali from nondescript kitchen sinks. Watching him, I remembered the day he found a gold chain tangled in the fibres of someone's excrement, and he wiped the excrement off against his corduroys and sold the chain at Nagin Pattni, and that evening, hoisted high upon his shoulders, he brought home the red Greatwall television. He set it in the corner of the sitting room and said, "Just look how it shines, as though it is not filled with shit inside."

And every day I plucked a bunch of carnations and snipped their stems diagonally and stood them in a glass bowl and placed the glass bowl on top of the television so that my father would not think of shit while he watched the evening news.

I said to Bwibo, "We have to send him back."

Bwibo said, "The liver you have asked for is the one you eat."

"But I did not really want him back, I just wanted to see his head."

Bwibo said, "In the end, he came back to you and that should account for something, should it not?"

Perhaps my father's return accounted for nothing but the fact that the house already smelt like him – of burnt lentils and melting fingernails and the bark of bitter quinine and the sourness of wet rags dabbing at broken cigarette tips.

I threw things at my father; garlic, incense, salt, pork, and when none of that repelled him, I asked Father Ignatius to bless the house. He brought a vial of holy water, and he sprinkled it in every room, sprinkled it over my father. Father Ignatius said that I would need further protection, but that I would have to write him a cheque first.

One day I was buying roast maize in the street corner when the vendor said to me, "Is it true what the vegetable-sellers are saying, that you finally found a man to love you but will not let him through your door?"

That evening, I invited my father inside. We sat side by side on the fold-away sofa, and watched as a fly crawled up the dusty screen between the grill and the window glass. It buzzed a little as it climbed. The ceiling fan creaked, and it threw shadows across the corridor floor. The shadows leapt high and mounted doors and peered through the air vents in the walls.

The wind upset a cup. For a few seconds, the cup lay lopsided on the windowsill. Then it rolled on its side and scurried across the floor. I pulled at the latch, fastened the window shut. The wind grazed the glass with its wet lips. It left a trail of dust and saliva, and the saliva dribbled down slowly to the edge of the glass. The wind had a slobbery mouth. Soon its saliva had covered the entire window, covered it until the rosemary brushwood outside the window became blurry. The jacaranda outside stooped low, scratched the roof. In the next room, doors and windows banged.

I looked at my father. He was something at once strange and familiar, at once enthralling and frightening – he was the brittle, chipped handle of a ceramic tea mug, and he was the cold yellow stare of an owl.

My father touched my hand ever so lightly, so gently, as though afraid that I would flinch and pull my hand away. I did not dare lift my eyes, but he touched my chin and tipped it upwards so that I had no choice but to look at him.

I remembered a time when I was a little child, when I stared into my father's eyes in much the same way. In them I saw shapes; a drunken, talentless conglomerate of circles and triangles and squares. I had wondered how those shapes had got inside my father's eyes. I had imagined that he sat down at the table, cut out glossy figures from colouring books, slathered them with glue, and stuck them inside his eyes so that they made rummy, haphazard collages in his irises.

My father said, "Would you happen to have some tea, Simbi?"

I brought some, and he asked if his old friend Pius Obote still came by the house on Saturdays, still brought groundnut soup and pumpkin leaves and a heap of letters that he had picked up from the post office.

I said, "Pius Obote has been dead for four years."

My father pushed his cup away. He said, "If you do not want me here drinking your tea, just say so, instead of killing-killing people with your mouth."

My father was silent for a while, grieving this man Pius Obote whose name had always made me think of knees banging against each other. Pius Obote used to blink a lot. Once, he fished inside his pocket for a biro and instead withdrew a chicken bone, still red and moist.

My father said to me, "I have seen you. You have offered me tea. I will go now."

"Where will you go?"

"I will find a job in a town far from here. Maybe Eldoret. I used to have people there."

I said, "Maybe you could stay here for a couple of days, Baba."

Okwiri Oduor was born in Nairobi, Kenya. Her novella The Dream Chasers *was highly commended in the Commonwealth Book Prize 2012. Her work has appeared, or is forthcoming, in* The New Inquiry, Kwani?, Saraba, FEMRITE, *and* African Writing Online. *She recently directed the inaugural Writivism Festival in Kampala, Uganda. She teaches creative writing to young girls at her alma mater in Nairobi, and is currently working on her first full-length novel.*

Choke

Jayne Bauling

Sometimes the wafer sticks to the roof of her mouth after she has received it from Father Phetho. It happens when she's waiting for Ntaba to come round with the wine. Father Phetho clings to the old ways and won't allow dipping. Would it make a difference if he did? The small white disc is so insubstantial it should dissolve easily and instantly without benefit of the stingy sip of wine that is all Ntaba grants. The fault must be hers when it sticks.

She would prefer dipping to sipping. Many of them would. There are rumours about the things you can catch, sipping. Some of them requested dipping last winter. That bad flu, children sent home from school, their parents re-infecting them and each other. Employers getting impatient if you were sick too long, or sick again, so people kept going in to work, but the teachers didn't want the children at school.

"Such ignorance," Father Phetho's wife, Zotha, said, dispatched to show them their error. "Don't you know germs can't survive on silver? And haven't you seen how carefully our dear brother Ntaba wipes the rim of the cup after each of you has drunk from it?"

With a blindingly white hand-hemmed piece of linen always perfectly laundered and ironed by Zotha herself as sacristan. And yes, the deep cup was silver, a gift from a richer parish in the diocese.

This is different. Elihle has worked the flavourless wafer well into her mouth. It should be easy, but she cannot swallow it. Ntaba has come with the shining silver cup, barely tilting it, grudging the congregation what he cannot have as he is recovering, or perhaps (if she's charitable) fearing that too much will lead them to addiction. Still she cannot get the wafer down.

Or the wine, glimpsed glowing red in the silver depths of the cup before Ntaba snatches it away.

It's not as if she's sick, queasy the way she was when the children were coming. Then it was her stomach rising in revolt and a revulsion in her mind, answering the message of her nose and eyes, stopping her from swallowing the coffee, the milky tea, the too-rich stew.

This comes from another part of her, a place she cannot identify. Unless it comes from outside of her?

She doesn't know.

She holds the wine and wafer in her mouth as she rises, using her hands on the altar rail to push herself to her feet. Walking back to her pew, she keeps her eyes down, as she has done since Makhi stopped coming home, stopped turning up for work, and all the standard enquiries have failed to find him.

The wine has made a small pulp of the wafer but both remain in her mouth. Seated, she snatches up her handbag from beneath the seat in front – scrabbles for a tissue – gets it to her mouth – pretends a coughing fit.

It becomes real, sharp tears springing to her eyes. Returning to the pew after her, her neighbour pats at her shoulder, offering comfort.

Elihle spreads her hands, making them big so that none can see the wine staining the white tissue, turning it pink. Mouth emptied, she hurries to hide the evidence in her bag.

"... we thank you for feeding us in these holy mysteries with the body and blood ..."

When the service is over, she doesn't linger in the aisle to greet. Probably no one expects it. It is another thing that has changed since Makhi stopping coming home. Every week she hurries out, face lowered. She is ashamed of the deterioration of the black and white outfit that marks her as Anglican. Frayed patches in the white, dust and a shine to the black.

Some items are easier. She chooses the small tins of tomato pilchards, even if it means she must do this more often. Weight is important too, packs of two-minute noodles, boxes with three or four sachets of instant soup, the smallest packets of teabags, all weighing almost nothing, easily stowed.

Experience has turned her adept. She dresses for these excursions in loose garments with big pockets and carries a bag she can open and close with a minimum of movement. Every action needs to look natural, the furtive as likely to attract attention as anything too bold.

Her heart is hammering hard and fast, hurting her as she approaches the tills with the bread, but she knows the most dangerous moments will come as she is leaving the supermarket. They have a new system now, a flashing number that is repeated by a recorded voice. It means she can't choose her till and avoid those staff members who might remember her from when she worked in the mall and shopped here most days.

She doesn't like coming to the mall, but it is close to her Monday piece-work here in the big town and she needs to rotate the shops. If she should become familiar and someone notices what is happening – or is she just one of many? She remembers those two high school girls, nearly in tears when they approached her.

"We've taken stuff, Mama, it's in our bags, but now we're scared they're watch-ing us. We want to put it back on a shelf. Can't you stand in front of us with your trolley so they don't see?"

She was angry with them. Righteously.

"Just put it back, they can't do anything to you unless you try to leave the shop with whatever it is. Don't involve me in your wrong-doing, and don't do it again."

That was before, when she could shop with a trolley and fill it; when she could exclaim indignantly at prices but still add the offending items to the trolley. When there were two salaries and her tips.

How would she answer them now? Only they wouldn't ask her today. With-out a trolley, with her former bulk melting from her bones, she can serve as no one's shield.

Fortune is with her. The woman on her till is unfamiliar.

Then the walk from till to exit, handbag pressed tightly to her side. Sweat springs up along her hairline and the plastic bag with the bread is slippery in her hand.

Outside. No voice, no hand stopping her, but relief is a thin, unsatisfactory thing. She feels ill. Once she strode through places like this and others gave way. Now she scuttles, she scurries, keeping out of the paths of others.

The hairdressers where she worked is now an optometrists. When she started, it was making coffee and sweeping up cut hair. Then she got to do the shampooing. The tannies liked her massaging fingers and tipped her well. Her boss talked about ethnic hair and said she could advise, but the ethnic hair, the younger women and girls, the men, all made their appointments at the big place with the products in the window where they also did manicures. That place is still here in the mall, doing good business.

"Overheads," her boss said after the mall's big revamp. "I'm setting up at home, doing the shampooing myself. Sorry."

"Sorry," they said when she asked at the other place, showing them the testimonial from her boss.

All in the same month that Makhi didn't come home. It never leaves her. Did something happen or did he choose? The possibility that he chose is what bows her head, lowers her eyes, so that strangers won't see and know.

On the bus home her stomach growls emptily, but there is no pleasurable anticipation to be had from the thought of the tins and packets in her bag and pockets.

She will eat bread. Again. It was bread in the middle of the morning, the only break she is permitted at her Monday cleaning job. It will be the same when she goes there on Friday. The Wednesday work is better. They tell her she can eat any leftovers in the fridge or take them home with her. There is always something. The Saturday morning man with the flat is best and worst. He gives her extra money for food, the times he doesn't say, "I don't have any cash on me, and I'm in a rush. But you ate at home, right? And you're only here for a couple of hours."

Her children don't know.

"Always the same food," her daughter complains when she gives them their plates.

"It's all we can afford until I get more work."

"Loser."

Elihle suppresses her resentment at the extra monthly expense since the girl started menstruating. Her daughter has grown aggressive, blaming her for her father's absence. The boy is mostly silent, his way of hiding hurt and hunger.

It is the youngest who cries for her father. She hasn't yet learnt deception or denial. If she is hungry she says so. She is often hungry.

"Your children no longer attend Children's Church, I noticed," Zotha says at Bible study on Tuesday night.

"My daughter," she mumbles. "A difficult age."

"I can talk to her. Or I can ask the rector."

It is always the rector or Father Phetho, never just Phetho. Occasionally it is my husband.

Elihle is always tired at the end of a Tuesday. With no piece-work for this day, she spends it looking. Buzzing at complex gates, knocking on doors, calling over walls. Domestic workers and gardeners look at her with pity or scorn, sometimes with suspicion. Dogs bark.

Her mind is pale, emptied out with tiredness. Her feet ache.

But there is food at the rectory.

It is not really Bible study since Zotha told Ntaba she was taking over and that the sessions would be held at the rectory in future. That was after she lost her place on the church council because some people wrote to the bishop complaining that she had held her position for seven years. She had also been a churchwarden twice, two terms of three years each with no break between. The writers were the same people who requested dipping instead of sipping. The bishop sent the archdeacon just before the annual vestry meeting. To give them some guidance, he said.

Zotha is too holy to hate, probably the holiest person in the parish next to her husband, but she has a lot to say about the archdeacon these days. She has had to find new ways of being active and in charge of the life of the church.

Understanding the Liturgy is the name of the course that has taken the place of Bible study. Zotha calls their sessions discussion groups, but mostly they consist of Zotha expounding on the meaning of different parts of the service. The dwindling group's occasional questions only reveal their ignorance, it seems. Tonight she is talking about the Penitence.

"You will have noticed how strict the rector is." Zotha is approving. "Those who come so late that they miss the Penitence are not permitted to receive the Eucharist."

"Why?" It is the only man attending who asks.

Zotha seems to swell a little as she prepares to answer him.

"How can you expect to partake of our Lord's body and blood if you haven't repented of your sins? And we are all sinners."

Elihle leans forward. Usually she is silent at these gatherings, but this is something that troubles her.

"What if we sin again after we have confessed and received the sacrament?"

Zotha's smile is meant to be kindly, Elihle is sure, but she finds it frightening.

"We are human, my sister. If we fall, we confess and try again."

"But if someone confesses and receives, knowing he will sin again?" she persists over her strong inclination to shrink back into her chair and become a mere observer.

Zotha swells a lot this time. It's the deep, indignant inhalation that does it.

"You know very well the words the rector says after we have confessed. Almighty God, who forgives all who truly repent … Truly, do you hear? Our confession would be an empty thing – worse, an unspeakable sin, if we make it with the intention of continuing to sin. To then accept the Eucharist would be an abomination. You should know this."

Someone wants to know where this leaves adulterers. Zotha reserves her special wrath for sins involving sex, and Elihle is relieved to lose her attention.

Tea and eats are always laid out on a hand-crocheted cloth covering the rectory's big dining-room table. Some Tuesdays Zotha will have been baking, but on others she likes to make a virtue of being too busy, a slave to the demands and duties of being the rector's wife.

Tonight's cakes and savoury snacks are bought.

"A funeral today, another tomorrow. Supporting my husband through weeks like these takes precedence over everything else," Zotha excuses herself, and her rueful sigh doesn't fool anyone. "What would we do without Woolworths?"

There is a Woolworths in the mall in the big town, but Elihle has never braved it except to walk through the clothing section, wishing.

The food looks expensive and there is plenty of it. Everyone is piling their little plates with an assortment. She does too. She helps herself to extra paper napkins, fancy patterned ones, never plain white. She will use them to wrap up some of the firmer treats, ready to slide into her bag when she is sure no one will notice.

She has learnt the trick from other church functions – from those she used to despise, spying them doing it and finding their greed undignified.

Greed. Need.

It happens again.

The words of the Penitence boom in her head as if there's a powerful microphone in there.

"... forgive us all that is past ..."

Past.

The Communion. "We do not presume to come to this your table ..."

Presume.

She thinks of that other church near the small house she fears they might soon have to lose if they don't find Makhi, if he doesn't come home and get his job back. The church where services are held in a big blue and white marquee. She has heard it's not about the Eucharist there.

Healing and salvation, they say.

Buying salvation, others claim, Zotha among them.

They go on longer, finishing later than the Anglicans, so Elihle is often home in time to see the armoured van arriving to fetch the morning's takings.

Even if she could afford to attend such a church, the Eucharist has always been central. She grew up with it, it has been the focus of all her Sundays, although it is only lately that she has given it her deeper thought.

The disc in her mouth, the wine. She gags, turning it into a choking fit, spluttering into another tissue when she gets back to her pew.

"Still coughing, sisi?" her neighbour says. "Maybe a doctor, nê?"

Every Sunday.

She absents herself only once. To miss a second week will bring a call, even a visit, from Zotha.

Remaining in the pew when everyone else is going up to the altar will cause talk. There is enough talk already, questions about Makhi.

"The incense," she blames when someone asks if she is ill.

It is the obvious scapegoat because members of the congregation have fainted before now when the young acolyte responsible is too enthusiastic.

"... this bread and this cup," Father Phetho intones under Zotha's approving gaze, "giving thanks that you have made us worthy ..."

Elihle doesn't say amen. Later, after she has choked into her tissue, they sing her favourite hymn.

"Bayete, bayete Nkosi ..."

She mouths the words, forces herself to clap and sway, but it doesn't fill her the way it did before.

Nothing fills her now. Not bread. Not the Tuesday night cupcakes and sausage rolls.

It is the mall's turn again. It has come round too quickly.

She is hungry.

There is no longer any need to choose loose clothing. Every garment hangs off her.

She walks through the Woolworths clothing section because it is quiet and cool there. The lingerie area attracts her. It is so long since she had new underwear. She needs a smaller size.

And her children need too, shoes for the boy, and the world for her daughter because want is need in the lives of high school girls. The little one's needs are simplest.

Her stomach complains, grumbling lengthily. There will be bread later, pilchards and beans for the children if her luck holds. Tomorrow night at the rectory – Zotha's baking perhaps, or treats from the food market Elihle has never entered because the flowers and pot plants and fancy boxes and tins at the entrance make her think there might be nothing sensible on the shelves beyond.

She isn't sure what makes her dare it today. Just to look.

It is quiet in the middle of a Monday afternoon. Two mothers with toddlers and a tall young man filling his basket with packets of croissants, nothing else. Maybe he runs a bed-and-breakfast.

Someone familiar, glimpsed and gone. Elihle turns her attention to the refrigerated section at the far end of the food market. How can margarine cost so much? And the cheese? She shakes her head and turns away.

The familiar figure again, down the aisle where the sweet things are. Rusks, biscuits, cakes, muffins.

Zotha.

Cramming cellophane-wrapped trays of little cupcakes into her immense black handbag and snapping it shut. A loaf of bread in her basket.

Elihle stares. Zotha doesn't notice her. She is intent on the biscuits now.

Understanding sweeps away incredulity. Elihle glides from the end of the aisle and ducks down the next one. She is laughing, but she must hold the laughter caught in her mouth for fear Zotha hears her through the shelves between them.

The way she has held the wafer and the wine for so many weeks. Choking on them.

She rushes from the food market. The laughter escapes her as she reaches the children's clothing section. It feels good, the first laughter since Makhi stopped coming home.

It is laughter she brings with her to the rectory on Tuesday night, silenced but still quivering there between her heart and stomach as she stuffs herself with the little cupcakes Zotha is offering.

Laughter she brings to the altar on Sunday.

Jayne Bauling lives in White River, Mpumulanga and is the author of 20 published novels. Her Young Adult novel E. Eights *won the 2009 Macmillan Writer's Prize for Africa, while* Stepping Solo *was awarded the 2011 Maskew Miller Longman Literature Award and* Dreaming of Light *won the Sanlam Gold Prize in 2012. She has had short stories included in* The Bed Book of Short Stories *published by Modjaji Books,* The Edge of Things *(Dye Hard Press),* African Pens 2011 *and two of the annual* Breaking the Silence *anthologies brought out by People Opposing Women Abuse and published by Jacana.*

Chicken

Efemia Chela

I

It was a departure of sorts, last time I saw them. Or maybe not at all. I had left sigh by sigh, breath by breath over the years. By the time my leaving party came, I was somewhere else entirely. From this place, I watched fairy lights being looped low over long tables and rose bushes being pruned. The matching china came out with the crystal glasses. The guards in our gated community were paid off to pre-empt noise complaints, as were the local police. Our racist neighbours were invited in time for them to book a night away. A credit card and a note on the fridge told me to go and buy a new dress ("At least knee-length, Kaba!!").

The entire dusty front yard was swept. Forthright, our maid, swept it once from the middle to the left and once from the middle to the right ensuring even distribution. She minced around the edges of the yard until she reached the right spot. Then she lovingly gave the earth a centre parting, like she was doing the hair of the daughter she seldom saw. Deftly, she made concentric circles with the rake, making certain not to be backed into a corner as she was in life. Paving would have been more in line with the style of the double storey house, the stiff mahogany headboard in my parents' bedroom and the greedy water feature in the atrium. "From the dust we came and to it we return," my father said cryptically whenever anyone asked why. Our relatives whispered in covens that BaBasil should have gotten 'crazy paving'. They were adept at spending money that wasn't theirs and would never be, due to equal measures of indolence and bad luck.

The same relatives called me down to some new-found duty. I slouched my way to them and despaired again that these women would never know me as an equal. Instead, I was a comedic interlude breaking up days of haggling in markets, turning smelly offal into scrumptious delicacies, hand-washing thin and dim-coloured children's clothes, and serving dinner to their husbands on knees that could grate cheese. I pitied them too much to be truly angry.

Celebrations transformed them into long-lost gods and goddesses. We enticed them with Baker's Assorted biscuits, school shoes and endless pots of tea. They descended from the village and came to town. Sacrifices were made; I

kissed most of my haircare products and magazines goodbye. But it was worth it
even though they were near strangers tied to us by nothing more than genetics,
a sense of duty and vague sentimentality. Who else could pound fufu for hours
without complaint until it reached the correct unctuous and delightfully gloopy
texture that Sister Constance demanded? Uncle Samu, my mother's brother
had driven away his third wife with a steady rain of vomit and beatings. As the
family's best drunk he could play palm-wine sommelier. His bathtub brew was
mockingly clear. Getting drunk on it felt like being mugged. And by midnight he
and Mma Virginia, who according to family legend were kissing cousins in the
literal and sordid sense, could always be counted on to break out 'The Electric
Slide' to the entertainment of everyone watching.

My aunties' voices rang out from a corner of the garden that had escaped my
mother's plot to turn it into a surburban Tuscan nightmare. I weaved between
the tacky replicas of Greek statues I had studied at university. The statues bulged
like marble tumors from the lawn. A brown sea snail slid round The Boxer's
temple. A rogue feather blew past Venus in the wind. Sister Constance smacked
her lips against her remaining teeth in disgust, "You took so long. They spoil
you-o!" I didn't reply and just contorted my features into what I thought was
penance and respect. "Let them have this," I thought. "They'll let me go soon."
After all, my mother, if she heard I had been too insolent, was far worse than all
of them combined.

They told me to kill them – three plain white chickens. Expressionless and
unsuspecting, they pecked the air while I shuddered above them, a wavering
shadow. I searched myself for strength and violence while rolling up the sleeves
of my blue Paul Smith shirt. "I guess I'll have to kiss this goodbye too," I thought
glumly. I was about to look like an extra who found themselves in the wrong
place at the wrong time in a Quentin Tarantino film. I curled my sweaty fingers
around a knife that someone had pressed into my right hand. I remember thinking how blunt it seemed; inappropriate for the task ahead. But then I grabbed a
chicken and felt its frailty.

"Wring and cut, Kaba. Wring and cut!" someone shouted.

I was too queasy an executioner. My shaking exacerbated the death flapping of the fowls and their blood spurts. I kept going. One. Two. Three. Gone in a couple of minutes. I barely heard the meat hitting the silver-bottomed tub. I was roused from my trance by the glee-creased face of Aunt Lovemore. As I tried to make my way to a shower, one shirt sleeve dripping, my mind emptied and all that remained was something someone once said to me or maybe... I couldn't tell where it was from. I still can't tell. It was:

"so much depends
upon

a red wheel
barrow

glazed with rain
water

beside the white
chickens."

The feast was that night. I looked at myself in the back of a serving spoon that had some stray grains of white rice smeared on it. No one would need it. Who could be bothered with Basmati when there was kenke to be unwrapped from wilted banana leaves like a present? When nshima so soft and personable was at the serving table in a large white quivering pile just waiting for some kapenta and an eager palate to come by? No, the Basmati would be given to the beggars who came by in the morning and expected nothing less from one of the town's richest families. Our generosity fostered expensive tastes.

My parents' cross-cultural marriage made for an exciting culinary event. From my father's side came slow-cooked beef shin in a giant dented tin pot. Simply done, relying only on the innate flavour of the marbled red cubes of flesh and thinly sliced onion getting to know each other for hours. It was smoked by open charcoal fire and lightly seasoned with nothing but the flecks of salty sweat from nervy Auntie Nchimunya constantly leaning over the steaming pot. Mushrooms were cooked as simply as Sister Chanda's existence. Fungi was hoped for in the night and foraged for at dawn. My favourites were curly-edged, red on top with a yellow underskirt and fried in butter. My lip curled as someone passed me a bowl of uisashi, wild greens and peanuts mashed into a bitty green mess. Little cousins cheekily defied their rank and begged for the prized parsons' noses from the grilled chickens. My chickens. Their shiny mouths indicated they'd already had more than enough chicken for the night and their age. Tauntingly, I popped one of the tails into my mouth and refused to pass them the crammed tray.

My mother, desperate not to be upstaged by her husband, reminded us all of her issue. The Fante chief's daughter, swathed in kente brought kontombire. It was a swamp-like spinach stew flooded with palm oil, thickened with egusi, specked with smoked mackerel and quartered hard-boiled eggs. It was carried to the table by three people, in a boat-shaped wood tureen from our mezzanine kitchen and the ancient forests of Ghana. Even her mother-in-law was impressed. She unwrinkled her forehead and loosened her fists a little, revealing her fingers stained so yellow by the sauce. From behind my thick pane of one-way glass, I saw my uncle had a bit of red garden egg stuck in his beard, but munched along cheerily, stopping briefly only to push round glasses up the bridge of his Ampapata nose. He was ignoring his side of waakye. I was tempted to take it and scoff it myself but then I looked down, remembering the chunk of succulent grasscutter that I'd pinched from Ma Virginia's bowl of light soup, still slightly hairy with a bit of gristle dangling from it. She was busy scanning the party for Uncle Samu's characteristic beaten-in black fedora. Grasscutter, fried okra and plantain. Now that would be tasty.

The chair to my left was empty but I preferred it to the barrage of information about my 30-year-old cousin's upcoming wedding, courtesy of our great-grandmother on my right.

"Bridget is off the shelf! Ow-oh!

"Praise God! The glory is all yours, Jesus!

"She's so fat and in all the wrong places. Oh! And she insists on this mumbling. Gah! And the boys just weren't coming, you know. So many weddings she had to see and cry at but no one was crying for her.

"Ei! You know you guys, you're just like their parents. You go abroad to these cold places where money is supposed to grow on trees. Even though there is no sun. You marry these white girls and boys who would die during our dry season, they are so thin. All bones. You get kept over there and we just hear news. Small-small news. And that you're making it big out there, with our name. But never come back. Oh God!

"But luckily this one never left. Just did what he was told to. A job, at least. Nothing much. But in the government, filing papers and not even important ones. So he will never get on the party's bad side like my brother did in the 60s. Eh-eh! No we can't have all that trouble again. Even though, God-willing we would recover.

"Now I can say all my girls are settled. Uh-huh! I can die now. Someone else is responsible for them now. They will do as I did. They will live as I lived. I have made them so. I have taught them well. They will never lose themselves. That is enough. Yes. That is enough. What other claim does a wife have?"

A chitenge-covered desk beside the second buffet table was for the DJ. There was a stack of records and the glow of a MacBook illuminated my older brother's face. He played eclectically, switched from computer to record player. Computer to Supermalt. Supermalt to record player. Mostly high life, with Earth, Wind and Fire, Glen Miller and Elton John. The musical liturgy of the family. Everything he knew would please. Near the bottom of the pile of records I saw a tiny snail that had escaped being stewed, creeping slowly upside down on the underside of a WITCH LP.

The fairy lights doused everyone in a soft glow. I think I was happy dancing with my little niece in the dust to the music; my heels forgotten by the hedge. Our yard was crowded and noisy until the sun came up. When I woke up in the afternoon, the noise echoed and resonated within me. It had embossed my inner ear. I'd captured it all. My brother had mentioned once that the earth was a conductor of acoustical resonance. If it's true, maybe the same goes for people. The night played over and over again. I was there shrouded by night. I looked around the garden with moistened eyes, a bulb of white wine condensing in my hand. I saw growing piles of soiled dishes whisked away by staff. Cutlery gleaming like silver bones under the moonlight. The people, the scale, the grandeur. It wasn't really anything to do with me at all.

II

I never wanted to admit it to anyone, but times were tough. I'd just left university with a distinction no one asked about. I barely managed to convince someone to hire me. Employers thought eight years of tertiary studies had left a gaping hole where experience should have been. In the year that the markets crashed, I was assured that the crisis would have sorted itself out by the time I entered the job market. It was nothing like that. I probably should have studied something more practical, but stubbornly I believed in my research. That there was really a place in the world for what I believed in.

I rented a room in the bum end of town and there I plotted my future. I played clairvoyant, gazing over my neighbours' corrugated iron roofs into the cavernous eyes of the mountain. Those were abrasive mornings. I tried to ignore the strangers in the abandoned lot opposite my window. Girls returned there the morning after the fact, looking for their dignity in the dirt or lost plastic chandelier earrings. Boys sprayed their scent on the crumbling wall, eyes on the lookout for scrap metal. The train rattled by, creaking as if each stop would be its last. Sometimes it was. I was late to work often. Gaudy prostitutes swooped indoors like vampires at first glimpse of the rising sun and the garbage men, part-time fathers of their children.

My relationship with my parents festered. I could expect disapproving text messages and automatic EFTs into my account. They sent me a pittance for rent and over the years had made sure to cultivate the kind of unspoken relationship that meant I wouldn't dare to ask for more money. Every ping in my inbox signaled another accusation. They told me that I was still young and there was still time to start a law degree. I baulked; their alms lessened.

I tried not to let their unpleasantness taint my days, curdle the sea I swam in or sharpen the wind. That coastal wind, a blustering soundtrack to my days in that seaside city. It pranked me in public, lifting my skirt. I, and undoubtedly others, got used to a flash of my thigh and untrimmed hedge creeping just past the edge of my briefs. I wasn't having enough sex to be greatly concerned with my appearance down there. Nothing in my top drawer could be rightly termed lingerie. In a town where everyone, through lies or privilege, was cooler and richer than you, I felt like I didn't even have to try. It was liberating. I went where my heart led me. Took tables for one. That's not to say I was starved for sex though. Every so often things would happen.

Like at this party one weekend. The party went down at a formerly whites-only pub which had been reclaimed, much like the word 'slut' had been some years before. "Oh my god! Eb! You little slut! I love you!" shrieked my friend, Alice, all arms and legs.

And at this moment, her arms were wrapped around the neck of her poly-amorous boything, Eb. His real name was Ebenezer, I think. I was embarrassed by black parents who still handed out Dickensian names to their children as if it would advance them up the hegemony. Though kudos to those kids too dark to blush called Aloysius and Enid for rebranding themselves as Loyo and Nida. The colonial pub, all flakey gilt frames and lined beige wallpaper tempered by dark woods, was full of them. Of us, I mean. Another generation tasked with saving Africa, yet ignoring the brief. Overwhelmed, we sought to please ourselves as best we could, whether that meant siphoning profits off family businesses, accepting scholarships overseas and never looking back or being assimilated into the incompetent state. Laughing, talking, smoking and dancing we could have been young people on any continent.

A girl and a boy sat down beside me and, after a perfunctory hello, asked me to join their threesome. Rather a forward approach, I thought, but then the boy backed out after I feigned some interest. He ran off.

"I think he's spooked. Sorry. I–" she said, trying to salvage the situation.

I raised my eyebrows in response and she leant towards me in a way that could only mean one thing. She led the intrepid exploration of my mouth with a gentle suction that left me gasping at once for air and more of her. I gripped her side. We ended up in my single bed. I wasn't dogmatic enough in my desire to be a lesbian but I liked the symmetry of being with a woman. Breast to breast. Gender didn't matter really anyway. I talked to Alice over coffee about it. I remember saying, "Boys. Girls. Whatever. We're always just two people searching... fumbling towards something."

Before she awoke, I surveyed her half-covered body. I was in awe as I always was when someone wanted to have sex with me. And then I saw it. Holding down her bottom lip with a finger, I tried not to wake her while getting a better look. It was an inner lip tattoo. God, it must have hurt – an egg. A single egg. I didn't have time to ponder what it meant. She woke and instantly seemed embarrassed. Not by her fevered cries that split the night or the way she had gushed a little between her legs when her body was racked with pleasure. She was embarrassed by the window edges taped shut to keep out the cold. The suitcase instead of a dresser. My crusty two-plate stove that I made nshima and beans on every day that it didn't short circuit the whole floor. She dressed in silence, turned away. When she did turn back, she looked at me, her eyes softened by pity. A bite of the lip said she hadn't realised what happened last night was a charity event. She scuffed her Converse on the rough floor as if trapped and bored.

"It-it was lovely," she said haltingly, trying not to meet my eyes again.

It was quiet for so long after that I nearly missed her squeak. "You might need this more than I do," she said, leaving R100, like a bird dropping, crumpled on the blue crate I called a nightstand. I didn't leave my room for two days after. The sheets trembled. But after my grief, I smoothed out what she thought I was worth and went and bought myself some fancy gin.

After that I worked harder at work than ever. I was one of 100 unpaid interns at the bottom of a global firm. Our only hope of getting hired was archiving gossip and evidence of affairs or theft amongst our superiors and using them as leverage once we became brave enough. I regret not being braver. My days went down the drain as I alphabetised contact lists and took coffee orders. I filed things. Then retrieved them for executives a couple of days later. Then was told to redo the filing system. One night I was given orders by one of the art directors. She was having a crisis, she said. Meaning, she was on a deadline and her coke-addled brain had no vision for the client's product. It was two days to the big pitch and she needed to "cleanse to create" so I had to rub all her erasers until I reached a clean surface on every inch of all 30 of them. Grumpily, I walked to her desk. First, I checked the pockets of the fawn-coloured jacket draped over her chair. I rustled for snacks, change or something to pep me up. Rustle. Rustle. But nothing. Except a business card. Rectangular and rounded at the edges, it read: Karama Adjaye Benin, Chief Recruiter, FutureChild Inc. The ovum bank you can trust.

III

I envied people who talked in certainties and absolutes. In plans and futures. I felt like I had nothing. Whether doubt, anger or hunger gnawed at my stomach became irrelevant. I set aside time at home to cry. I used the internet at work to find more jobs, but I was already stretched thin on that front. Sleep was for the in-between moments, wherever they fell. I lied my way into focus groups and market surveys for products I couldn't afford. My heels wore down. My gait changed. I saw myself in the blacked-out windows of a skyscraper en route to somewhere. At first I didn't realise who the hurried girl with the hunched back was. I looked again. She looked hunted.

I had to stay home trying to keep warm or risk having to party sober. I could coast through end-of-the-month weekend when everyone was generous at the bar or people threw parties at houses with cellars and drinks cabinets. Sometimes at clubs like The Pound, I let old men call me a doll and dribble nonsense in my ear over synth beats and the squeak of pleather. I listened, smiled and was intermittently witty, but generally I only spoke to say, "Double Jack, please."

They were men who lived on promises. I starved on hope. This was fourth-wave feminism.

I considered prostitution quite seriously after that one night stand with Ananda. The concept didn't seem so far-fetched any more. In a way, the business card was my chance. Their offices were in an innocuous looking building not far from the CBD. It was difficult to know what to wear, but I wanted to look like someone who deserved to be reproduced. I looked nervously out the window at the wet mist blurring anyone who had the temerity to leave the house. I picked my most ironed dress and a smart jacket and took a hardback book to read. This choice too was the source of some anguish as it needed to be big enough to hide my face in case I saw someone I knew, but also had to double as a tool to intrigue and impress the recruiter. My father had always said *Ulysses* would come in handy someday. I was angry that he was right.

The chrome chair felt sterile and sharp against my body. I looked around at the waiting room, gooey with pink branding about ethnically diverse angels, mama birds and dreams. All the framed stock photos were rosy assumptions of family life. I tried to concentrate on filling out the form handed to me. It was the only truth I had dealt with in a long time. I found it refreshing. I couldn't fail here. I was qualified to do this, to be a donor. I would get a bonus for every year of post-graduate study I had achieved. Checking all the details, I was glad my natural mediocrity had its uses – healthy, black, 65kg, brown-eyed woman. A non-smoking, 24 year old, with regular periods and taking no contraceptives. A little girl with pigtails and a pinafore smiled up at me from my lap. These photos would complete my personal zine, to be handed over to the agency for consideration. The girl was blissfully unaware of what was happening, just smiling shyly like she always would. I turned her over.

Why were the blank lines so easy when life was so hard? I looked so different on paper. Broken down into sections, I barely recognised myself. I felt that I had only ever heard of this woman, had never met her. I fake-read my book, which gave me time to really mull over what I was doing. I was sure it didn't matter. The eggs were just lying around inside of me going to waste on the twelfth of every month. From what I remembered from school, I had thousands of them in reserve. I was a veritable mine of genetic material. This is was nothing to cry over.

I signed my contract while lying on my back, during one of several ultrasounds. Injection by injection I began to think that it was meant to be. Maybe it was the hormones. The red-headed woman doing the extraction sacrificed congeniality for professionalism. I gathered that she wore all white, even outside work. The only thing that differentiated her from a robot was her revelation that she had also been a donor, albeit in her thirties.

"I was just young enough. I had a lot of bills. I wanted to give the gift of parenthood to someone less fortunate," she said, as if from a script.

To convey emotion, she punctuated her speech with weird bobs of the head. To make awkward conversation while doing my scans, she asked about my degree. I sensed misunderstanding. Sometime after third year, I had learnt to let the confusion pass without comment or justification. They'd see.

"Your ovaries are doing well."

A few months later I was forced to look up at her like I had several times before. Her whole face was like clingfilm, wrapped fast across sinew and bone. I squinted up, then dropped my head down, away from the scrutiny of the powerful lights. My neck slackened as I breathed in the gas. I lost consciousness counting backwards.

"You're a hero now," said Karama as I stumbled out, still a little woozy and anaesthetised. Trying to be kind, she crushed me into her body. I didn't feel like anyone's saviour, even though there were two red stigmata in my knickers. My phone beeped somewhere at the bottom of my bag letting me know that I had been paid. I ignored it.

After the extraction, I felt less lost. I knew exactly where I was and where I was going. I went home and climbed up the rickety fire escape to the roof, holding on fearfully to the rail afflicted with rust, making it wart-like to the touch. The cold mist cloaked me in damp as I stepped onto the crunchy pigeon shit roof. I stood motionless looking down at the swaddled city. I knew what was hidden below the mist. Shacks slanted with uncertainty. Six-lane highways and car ads clinging to billboards beside them. Wide boulevards bordered by alien trees and thin housewives in cafés. Narrow byways lined with needles. Underfunded primary schools with middle-aged men parked outside trying not to eat the sweets they used as bait. Cold modern apartment blocks; all light, expense and lack of privacy. Secret leisure houses cowering behind high walls. Leaning road signs waiting to be stolen by students.

All of these places. I would never know where my child would be. No, I would. I would always be beating paths for it to follow. It would wind its way around my brain. I'd stage shadow puppet shows on the walls of my skull, playing out its careers, hobbies and loves. One director, one spectator. I didn't want the child to be sheared between two lives, two minds, two imaginations. My own and its own. I pleaded to no one that they would spare it, not rip it apart. I hoped my ghost would not smother it. That my wishes would not hamper it. I prayed it wouldn't be pained. Or nagged by the phantom limb – the gnawing mystery of my existence. I wanted its parents to take all the credit. I hoped they would never tell it.

That my donation would just be fiction.

Efemia Chela is a 21-year-old writer with her body in Cape Town and her heart in Japan. She had a bumpy childhood in Zambia, England, Ghana, Botswana and South Africa. She is married to a film camera. They go everywhere together and have many square children. She gets her thrills from remotely attending international fashion weeks, artistic intertextuality, old movies and tasting new cuisines. The short story "Chicken" is her first published work.

Bloodline

Tarryn-Anne Anderson

Spirits on board the *Alma Lucie* are high as the sun begins to dip. Lizbet shifts in her seat to get more comfortable, angling herself so that the cabin roof shades her eyes. The boat is slow, but fast boats are light boats, and light boats mean light pockets.

"This catch is like back in the day," an old fisher says. "I remember when we used to catch like this every day. Six days a week, with only a break for Sunday service. Jirre, jong. Those were the good times."

Lizbet stares at the bow as it slices the water in two, carving a passage for the boat to follow home. The crew banter with one another. They tell jokes and tease one of the younger members about the girl he just started seeing. Lizbet doesn't know them well enough to join in, and they make no attempt to include her.

"Do you remember when ou Tommy lost his finger?" one says.

"We caught so many yellowtail that day, there wasn't a moment's rest!"

The old man goes on. "I was still a laaitie on board. I had just got my standard nine. Decided the sea life was for me. Tommy was just a bit older than me, but we started at the same time," he says, chuckling at the recollection. "That day the skipper, it was Oom Jackson that time, gave us each one line. It was in the days before we had this nylon. Fishers used to make their own bloodline. They'd strengthen it by rubbing it with sheep's blood. He gave us the line, and bait, and we put it in the water. We had no protection for our hands and must just battle with these big fish, pulling the line in our bare hands," he says.

"But nobody told you about putting something on your fingers?" a boy asks.

"Nee jong, they weren't so soft as we are with you now, hey. We had to learn the hard way how things were," another fisher added.

"Ja, I saw blood all over my hands," the old man says, "but I thought it was from the fish. Then there was a big bugger, and Tommy, it was his line that gave the temptation. There he bites! 'Yoooe!' shouts Tommy and then he starts to pull and pull, wrapping it round his hands so it won't slip. Next thing, zhoops! There he takes Tommy's finger. The line was so tight around Tommy's hands it cut it right off. There, into the sea to feed the fishes." A chuckle passes around, and he shakes his head. "Ja, those were good times."

"They weren't this cheerful this morning," Lizbet says to Abrie.

"They didn't believe we'd catch," he says, adjusting the steering slightly.

The main harbour wall is in front of the boat, flanked on either side by a pier which stretches out to meet a lighthouse – green on the left, and red to the right. The boat is hoisted close to the concrete and pulled in on heavy ropes. Two men jump ashore, each clearing the gathering crowd away from a small circle of space, which is simultaneously being filled with snoek. One fisherman picks up a fish and passes it, like a slippery rugby ball, to another, who then sends it gliding through the air to slap down on the accumulating pile on the concrete floor. All the while bidding is going on, hose pipes are rinsing down, and bait is being packed away. The gear is gathered together. It all happens quickly, with the fervour of men who want to be warm and dry, on land, with a quart of beer.

"Haai. There's too much here for me to sell. I'll give you ten rand a snoek," Maria says.

"Ten!" says Abrie, "You'll sell them for a hundred each."

"Not a hundred. No. And anyway I can't sell all of them today," she says.

"Fifty rands then. And if we came here with five you would say the same thing. There are two hundred fish here," he says.

"Yes, two hundred. Who can sell two hundred? Five I could sell, not two hundred. It's already past three. I'll give you ten a piece."

"There are other langaaners here, tannie. I can sell to them also."

"Ja, try mos. No one will give you more than ten," she replies.

"Fifteen," Abrie says.

"Twelve."

"Jirre! Fine," he says, "unload the rest." Abrie takes the handful of notes from her as her assistants transfer some of the snoek onto a plastic groundsheet and the remainder into an old shipping container that has been converted into a make-shift cooling room.

"Abrie," she says to him, "Once you get too good at finding fish, you might discover there's no more fish to find, hey."

He knows that there are already no fish to find. For weeks and weeks before they found the girl, his crew had been coming home empty-handed. When they did catch, it was done knowing that each one they took today was one they could not catch tomorrow. But then, it's hard to think about how few fish there will be next year if you are hungry today. And at least, Abrie thinks, none of his men will go hungry tonight. The same is not true for the other boats he can see coming in with catches that will barely be able to refill their fuel tanks, let alone their bellies.

He pays Lizbet an equal cut, despite her inability to catch any fish herself. She contributed in her own way, though his wife would cross herself to hear him speak of it. The girl is sitting on the edge of the dock in front of *Alma Lucie*'s stern, kicking at it with her worn shoes. She tucks the handful of cash into a pocket when he passes it to her. He thinks about offering her the use of their shower, because she really could use it. But he knows that she probably would not accept. His wife wouldn't like it anyway, and his reputation has suffered enough from just letting her on board.

"Can I sleep on the boat again tonight?" she asks.

"Ja, but not forever," he says. He found her in the hull two nights ago. She was sleeping on the old tarp they used for covering the fish. It was not the first time he'd seen her. She'd been hanging around the harbour for the past few weeks. His first instinct was to kick her off – far and fast – but there was something about the way she pleaded for a chance to prove herself that softened him. If he knew in advance how she'd do it, he might not have agreed. *But*, he thinks, *at least she seems to keep her distance from the other stragglers in the harbour who try to make a living by getting the seals to clap for scraps. That's something.*

Lizbet buys a warm parcel of fried fish, wrapped in white paper and drenched in vinegar. The smell of it on the wharf has been tempting her to the point of nausea for the past two weeks. She eats it on an up-ended crate tucked in a corner, and watches the langaaners packing up the fish market. Most of the fishers have gone now, and those that remain are already drunk. They revel in small groups along the periphery, the rotting fish smell of the harbour apparently more appealing to them than their wives.

As Lizbet lies in the cabin bunk that night she thinks about her first day at sea. The men were not happy to see her and not one greeted her, but they could not argue openly with their skipper. Outside a bottle breaks on the concrete and garbled expletives rise and fall like the waves. The boat knocks softly against its neighbour as it rocks in the night breeze, and the wooden boards murmur their soft creak to her as she falls asleep.

Lizbet swims through a murky dreamscape. Spears of light pierce the water around her and reach down towards the depths, suspending particles in their beams. The current consumes her and moves her forward. Shimmering silver and blue around her are fish, and they swim together, and she is one of them.

Then comes the man. He walks into the water and is swept on by the current. Around and around it spins him. His arms are flailing and his legs are kicking but he cannot reach the surface. She tries to reach out to him, to help him, but she cannot. She's a fish. He seems to know that she wants to help. He places his hand upon her side. The stream is filled with energy. The drowning man begins to swim more easily – gills have grown on the side of his neck. His arm is no longer on her. It has become a fin. His face, too, has begun to transform. His head becomes wide and flat, his eyes grow further and further apart. All that remains of the man are his legs, which kick out behind the body of a shark.

"Jirre. Aren't you going to get cold?" Abrie says with a smirk as she shuffles over, her arms barely able to touch her sides for the many layers of jersey she's wearing – every one she owns. He stands alone on the wall in the dark morning. The other fishermen give her a wide berth, but Abrie appears not to notice.

"It was freezing yesterday," Lizbet says. Crewmen linger outside the row of harbour storage rooms, smoking the last half of a leftover cigarette, the white smoke billowing out of their mouths in the cold.

The boat is reversed out of her docking bay, the rumbling engine adding wafts of diesel fumes to the smell of wet concrete and sea. She's steered in a half circle until the stern faces the mountains above sleepy Kalk Bay, and the left hand side of the boat is parallel with the wall of the harbour.

"Môre, môre," comes the call from the boat docked beside theirs.

"Khalid," Abrie greets.

"I hear you had a good day yesterday. Where'd you go?"

One of his crew, on board already, throws ropes across to be looped around the rusting yellow bolsters. Two other crew members catch these, and together they pull the boat close to the harbour wall so that gear can be loaded on board. Each man hops across the gap effortlessly, carrying flat cardboard boxes of bait.

"Ag, just so an hour and a half out towards Cape Point," Abrie says.

"There's no fish there," Khalid says.

"It's a struggle. We have to find new ways," he says. Khalid shakes his head and returns to his crew.

Later, Lizbet turns to Abrie and says over the stuttering hum of the boat engine, "Maybe some people don't like the new way."

As Abrie cuts the engine, the sea asserts itself. The swish and roll of the currents beneath the hull cause the boat to sway from side to side. Salt fills the air.

"How do you know we'll catch here?" she asks.

Abrie points to sleek dark shapes breaching in the waves just beyond the circle of light cast by the lamp. "Where there is seals there is fish," he says.

Lizbet straddles a bench, and leans over to dip her hand into the black water. The hairs on her arms are raised by goosebumps. Abrie gives her a single nod. There are no other boats around. The other crew members avert their eyes, shifting uncomfortably as she starts humming – a repeat performance with which they are not enamoured, despite having called the encore.

The sound consumes her. Everything but the back and forth rocking of the boat fades into the distance. All she can hear and smell and feel is the sea all around her. She throws herself further and further into the hum, letting it become her. Then she dips her hands back into the sea. The icy cold shudders up her arms, but she holds them there until they go numb. She can feel the movement of the water. It laps around her elbows and tickles her fingertips. She remembers her dream from the night before, and the man who swam beside her. She pictures the fish as well and imagines them swimming deep below.

The GPS-fishfinder bleeps softly, sporadically. A flutter of coloured dots appears on the small screen. Abrie studies the patterns the dots are making carefully. "Anchovy," he says to Lizbet, though she does not appear to notice.

Lizbet turns her mind to the smaller fish. She imagines schools of them, swimming far around the coast. Then she tries to imagine how she would call them if she too were a fish, as she had been the night before. Lizbet's song rises and falls with the boat. The frequency of the bleeping escalates. The display of blue dots on the screen becomes denser as the anchovy congregate under the boat.

She can feel the movement in the water shift with the movement of the many fish below it. She hums louder and deepens her tone to delve further. There, around the small fish, she can feel them swimming at the edges: snoek, but far away. Lizbet turns her mind back to the anchovy.

Abrie watches her intently, then switches his gaze back to the fishfinder as her hum transforms into something else. The activity on the boat picks up as Lizbet's song dies away. Each man is raking the top of the water with a small handheld net, scooping dead anchovy out of the water and dumping them in a large shared bucket.

"We are over the bait ball now," Abrie says, pointing at the blue dots on the screen.

Lizbet examines it. "Everything works together," she says. They watch as larger, more disparate dots begin to appear, moving more slowly. Without the large stock of anchovy, the snoek are forced to swim closer to the boat to get to the food. The ritual has drained Lizbet. She shifts herself into the small onboard cabin and down onto one of the two bunks to sleep it off.

For the first time, Lizbet's dream is different. The man stands on the bank of the Zambezi river. She recognises him from the water in her previous dream. "Besa," his wife says, "this is a dangerous pursuit. Your n/um may not sustain."

"It is the only way," he says.

"There are other ways, my love," she says. "I can go out with the women in the morning. We will find some food."

"We cannot continue like this. The lands are as dry as our nets are empty. This is a thing I can do. It is expected of me."

The man kisses his wife. Their small child lies in her arms. He returns to his work at the river bank, where he draws a red line down the rock into the water. "This line will connect me from this place to that." Along each side he creates a fringe of white dots. "And these are my footprints from here to there." Besa steps into the water, wading towards the stream. Then he dives under and lets God move him forward. All along the river bed he moves, swimming and kicking himself along with the current.

Lizbet is with him; his feelings are her feelings. Inside his chest his lungs burn and tighten. He knows that the fire inside him is a test. Electric fish swim all around him. He is drowning, but he does not know what to do. He reaches out to touch the fish, to acquire their potency, but he cannot. They swim by him and around him as he is carried along. A blackness creeps into his vision. He knows this will be the end. It was a foolish pursuit. Beside him swims another fish, this one closer than the rest and in time with him, not moving past and away. He thinks that maybe this one will work.

Tingling shocks run down his spine as the burning subsides and the water accepts him. Faster and faster he is able to go. The water shimmers around him. They swim for a long distance, until the water itself seems to have changed. What was once young is now old. He is no longer in the time and space of his wife and child, and he is no longer a man.

When Lizbet wakes up the morning sunlight has dissolved the fog, and the light gleams on the rippling surface of the still sea.

"Onsê gast is nou terug!" Abrie says to the rest of the crew.

"Come," he says. He walks along the benches to the stern of the boat: the place of honour for the boat's skipper. Taking out his gear box he motions for her to pick a sinker for his line, then shakes his head at her choice and points towards a lighter one.

"Good," he says as she hands it to him. Carefully, he begins to prepare the line, tying the hook and sinker in place and tugging at it to test its durability. He selects a sardine from the cardboard box next to him, and then chops the tail fin off. He threads the hook once through the flesh of the body, and then through the eye of the sardine.

After casting, Abrie pulls the line up again using the thumbs and forefingers on both of his hands, and then lets it down. He does this slowly, pulling up a bit, letting down a bit less, pulling up more, down less, searching through the current for a fish.

Lizbet busies herself with a line of her own. She baits and hooks it like Abrie taught her the day before.

"Vat hom korter en gooi hom verder," Abrie says to her as he watches her attempt at casting. She pulls the line up again and holds it closer to the sinker, throwing it out towards the back of the boat. It lands much further away this time. Abrie nods his approval, then adds, "Next time throw it up near the front, and let the current take the line down. Then it won't tangle with anyone else's."

On the opposite side of the boat a fisherman furiously wrenches his line from the water with both hands. Left and right he pulls it out of the sea, until the water breaks around the head of the snoek. Its skin has a black and green metallic sheen. Its gills flare as the man wrestles with it in his grip. He slips three fingers under its head into the soft pale flesh beneath. Then he rips upwards, breaking the jaw and snapping the neck. His plastic yellow overalls are slick with its blood as he tosses the fish into one of the foot holes.

"Today we will have a good catch," Abrie says.

A quiet descends as the attention shifts to the work at hand. Somewhere in the hull an object has come loose, and the boat clinks gently as it rocks. The piles of fish in each fisher's compartment is growing. They twitch as their fellows are tossed on top of them, necks newly snapped. Along the horizon the dark shapes of other boats are visible. Time passes slowly. The sun rises and dips. The boat sinks lower in the water, heavy with harvest.

The tedium is broken when a line snaps around lunchtime. Looking up at his fellows one fisher says, "Shark, probably." Abrie hooks and baits a thicker line. This he casts out from the front.

"Kyk hoe trek hy!"

"Jirre."

"Druk hom!"

Abrie wrests the fish from the water, pulling against the strength of the fish. A fin rears. He grabs the tail, just before the caudal fin, and lifts the thrashing sand shark out of the water. Abrie uses a short sharp knife to make two deep incisions down each side of the sand shark, just behind the gills. Then he throws it to one side of the boat to bleed out.

Thump. The shark's tail bangs against the deck. Thump. Thump. It thrashes its tail from side to side. Lizbet stares as it heaves, drowning in the open air.

"Can't you just kill it?" she asks. The blood seeps out in rhythmic pumps. It's only a fish she thinks to herself. Just a fish.

"You have to let it bleed out. The blood turns the meat sour if you kill the shark. You need the blood out when it dies," Abrie says.

"You eat shark?" Lizbet asks.

"Ja. You probably have also. They call it so 'Cape Whiting' up in the restaurants. Tastes just like hake. You wouldn't even know," he says. She feels that she would. Surely she would.

"We get good prices for shark," Abrie says.

"From the Chinks, maybe," says Lizbet.

The afternoon has only just passed when Abrie gives the call to pull up.

"Take it down to the hold," Abrie instructs one of the crew. The man lifts the sallow shark from its resting place and deposits it in an empty crate, which is then shoved into the hold to hide it from bedecked shoulder pads. The snoek they top with ice and cover with plastic sheets, like they did the day before.

Two men crank up the anchor. Those that have them are settling in with sandwiches. Someone has put the kettle on the old single plate gas stove that serves as a galley. Soon a weak but passably warm pot of tea is being passed around. It is only palatable with an excess of sugar. With a chugging grumble and a jolt the engine is started.

Lizbet has caught no fish. She was not able to recast her line. She sat and watched as the life dripped from the slits behind the shark's gills, and the tail ceased its thumping. Her heart burning. She was shocked by the violence of fishing on the first day that she came onboard. She witnessed the snapping of the necks and the pooling blood that smelled of salt and iron, and the thought occurred to her that fishing was more like hunting than she realised. But until now it had not felt like murder.

The first time Lizbet dreamt of the shark-man she was twelve. She was staying with her grandmother for a few weeks. The social worker said that it was "a psychological trauma resulting from the death of both parents," but her grandmother knew it was something quite different.

"My child," she said, "your parents have gone to join God, but you must not fear. In all families there is death, yes, but in ours there is also a strong connection between the living and the passed."

Lizbet did not, at first, understand what that meant. She struggled, night after night the same dream, with the drowning man. Then one evening, her grandmother told her a story. It was one that she had heard many years before, from her own mother: "A long time ago – many centuries back – our family lived on the Zambezi river. There were those who said that they used to be very good fishers. For many years they would catch and catch," she said as she braided Lizbet's hair for bed. "But as you know, even at this young age, hard times come. Sometimes the fish would go to other places that no-one would know of," round and round she looped the elastic band, securing the braid in place.

"A hard time like this came and the people did not know what to do. But in their village was a magic-man. One who could ask things from the animals. He had married your great-great-grandmother and he said he could help. One day he went to ask the fish where they went in the dry times. He left his wife and child behind to wait for him. She would stand on the bank each day, looking out. Looking for her husband who had gone with the water, waiting for him to return. But, he did not."

It was said, her grandmother told her, that the man had been taken down the Zambezi all the way to the ocean, and that the Agulhus had swept him to Cape Town. But no-one had been sure. "But your gift, young one, lets you speak to our ancestors. Now we know what became of him, we know that he was alright. He did not drown. The sea gave him a new home."

What her grandmother did not tell her was that many years later, when the magic-man's child had gone on to have children of her own, a storyteller visited their village. They asked him over and over again to tell stories into the night, and he did. But once he had run out of stories they still asked for more. So he told them a story that he had heard, which he thought could not be true. It was a story about an old cove where walkers had found the body of a half-man, half-shark, washed up on those shores. A long red line of blood ran down the beach toward the sea, connecting him from that place to this. Beside it were footprints, spots in the white sand.

A strong wind has picked up and Lizbet braces against it as they hammer over the choppy waves. The shark's blood coagulates under the soles of Lizbet's rubber boots. When they get to the harbour someone will hose it down. The blood will dissolve, and it will run watery-red back into the sea.

Tarryn-Anne Anderson lives in Cape Town, South Africa. She has a Master's degree in Social Anthropology from the University of Cape Town, where she conducted research among fishers in Kalk Bay. She drew on that experience for inspiration while writing this short story. She currently heads up the content team at Paperight, where she works to increase access to books. She also blogs about books, travel, and the veritable awesomeness of everyday life at animprobablefiction.com. You can find her on twitter @tarrynosaurus.

The Broken Pot

Dilman Dila

She could not sleep. Her stomach blazed with an emptiness that brought memories of her wedding cake, of the white crumbs that littered the red table, of the morning after when a column of ants carried them away. She wished she could shed tears, but her eyes were dry. Her throat was parched, her lips cracked, her tongue snaked out in search of food. She could taste the sweetish groundnut sauce her grandmother used to prepare when she was still a little girl.

Somebody struck a match and lit a tadooba. The candle filled the room with a sombre red light, with the odour of kerosene. Though she could not see the old woman's face, she knew it was her grandmother standing in the shadows when a wrinkled finger pointed at the tray of food. The bracelet on the hand, glowing like sunset, made her conscious that it was only a dream. She had finally drifted into sleep. Her granny urged her to devour the roast chicken smeared with odi, to gobble up the sour malakwang and sweet potatoes, to lick dek ngor off the clay pot. At first it felt like a happy dream, for what could be frightening about feasting on her beloved granny's food? Then the anger she had bottled up for three days erupted. She kicked the tray off the bed, so that food flew all over. She became fully awake when her husband turned on the light, showing her that there was no food, that her grandmother was twelve years dead, that the dream was an omen, a call from the other side. For the first time since she had decided not to eat until her husband declared his love for her, she realized that she might starve to death.

He sat beside her on the bed, scowling because she had interrupted his sleep. She did not look at him. She waited for him to ask her what was wrong, prayed that he would put a hand around her shoulder and assure her it was all a dream, that all this was not happening on their honeymoon. But he merely snapped off the light and went back to sleep.

The darkness swallowed her. Something roared in her ears, like a river raging over a cliff. The sound of hunger. When her eyes grew used to the gloom, she saw shapes, illusions of light and shadows. A pillar of flame flowed down from the ceiling and dissolved into a cloud at the foot of the bed. It was blue, burning with such brilliance that inside it she could see a tree, a big old tree bare of leaves. Its branches hung above the ground like limbs. Under the tree was her husband. He flirted with a rustic woman who had a basket on her head and a little boy on her back. She rubbed her eyes to get rid of the vision, but the after-image burned inside her skull. Her head ached.

She could not bear lying in the same bed with him anymore. The sound of his snoring, the heat from his body, the odour of his sweat, was suffocating her.

For the first time in three days, she crept from the bed. Her legs collapsed beneath her. She fell to the ground, banging her head against the bedside table, sending the lamp crashing to the floor. She heard him stir, and once again the explosion of light blinded her. She waited for him to say something, but he kept silent.

She rose to her feet heavily and limped to the door. Her hands trembled so badly that she could not open it. She felt his eyes burning into her back. She wished he would speak, ask her what was wrong, where she was going, but still he kept silent. He had not spoken either when she had asked him about the woman. The silence proved his guilt.

Yet, five days earlier she had thought that the silence proved the depth of his love for her, as he had waited for her at the altar with a ring in his palm. She walked down the aisle, her gown trailing over a carpet of rose petals. The veil hid her joyful smile. She walked slowly, in rhythm to the soft voices of a choir and the gentle clapping of the congregation, eyes fixed on him. He stood, as though unaware of the cheering people, unaware of the hundreds of candles lighting up the church or the statues of long dead gods watching them make their vows.

She opened the door and staggered into the semi-darkness of the short corridor. Four other doors led off the corridor. A mosquito buzzed above the roar of the river. She swayed like a drunkard, unsure of which door to open.

The first led into the living room. She could sleep on the couch where she had imagined they would spend so many happy evenings together, in front of the TV, drinking red wine, eating romantic dinners. She reached out to open the door, hesitated. She had avoided the living room since that morning, two days into their honeymoon, when she'd leapt out of bed to answer a knock at the door. They had planned to picnic at the lakeshore that day, the weather was perfect for such an outing. She was happy until she opened the door. No one was there. An envelope sat on the doormat. No addressee. Inside was a photo of a woman posing in front of a flowering shrub, smiling into the camera, a basket on her head, a baby strapped to her back... No. She could not go into the living room.

The second door led into the kitchen. She could smell the honey and odi on the shelves, the pork and chicken in the refrigerator. It made her nauseous. She did not want food or drink. She was on a hunger strike to force the truth out of her husband, to make him explain why he married her when he already had a child with someone else, a child young enough to have been conceived when they were dating.

The third door led to a second bedroom, but she was afraid to open it too. She had already decorated it for the children she hoped they would have. As she swayed, she could hear their laughter; a son, two daughters playing, throwing things around – a future she could not have anymore.

The fourth door was her only option. It led into the bathroom, a room free of pain. She staggered in. Her feet twitched in protest when they touched the cold tiles. Mosquitoes sung with such intensity that she believed they were trying to tell her something. Her body dragged itself to the tap against her will. She turned on the faucet. She shoved her mouth into the gushing water. It tasted like stale tea on her parched tongue. It hurt her cracked lips. The water ran into her hair and ruined her fancy bridal hairstyle. It entered her nose, flowed into her lungs, choked her. She turned away from the tap and took in long gulps of air. When her breathing had evened out, she resumed quenching her thirst. This time she avoided the tap and sucked the water off the floor. After she had drunk her fill, her head collapsed onto the cold tiles.

His cheating did not hurt as much as the whole world knowing, as much as people she called her best friends not telling her. She thought they must have been mocking her, laughing at her, when they had clapped and cheered on her wedding day. They must have been singing about her stupidity to wear a gown for a man who was in love with someone else.

Even her boss had known. Why had he not said anything when she handed in her resignation? He had only smiled, showing off his teeth to reveal how lowly he thought her. She had worked up north, eight hours on the bus from her new home in the city. She wanted the marriage to work more than she wanted a career. She quit, hoping to find a new job, though she knew she could never get a job as good as the one she had had. The city was full of desperate jobseekers, a thousand overqualified people fighting for a single, poorly paid position. She had thrown her career away to dedicate the rest of her life to her husband. She did not have regrets then, even after she had spent all her money paying for the wedding. She had wanted it to be the happiest day of her life. She'd had no regrets until she found the photo.

Starving was a slow, painful way to go. The problem with swallowing pills, or using a rope, or drowning, was that it gave him no chance to tell her the truth. To explain who the people in the photograph were. All she wanted was for him to say that he loved her, that he had always loved her, would always love her, that he had made a mistake and the people in the photo were just that, people in a photo who did not mean anything to him, and never would. That was what she wanted to hear.

But all he did was berate her for being overly emotional, even irrational, for blowing the photograph out of proportion, giving it a meaning it did not have. He said that her 'stupid jealousy' would ruin their marriage. But he did not say what she wanted to hear. Instead, he lost patience. He stopped talking to her. Their honeymoon dissolved into pain and silence.

He kept silent, though he knew she would not eat unless he opened his mouth. He kept silent as though he wanted her to die.

She felt, more than saw, him walk into the bathroom. She felt his bare feet in the water, the same water in which she lay. She heard him sit on the toilet bowl, could imagine his chin in his palm as he pondered what to do with her, his sulky wife sprawled out on the bathroom floor.

"Talk to me," she said, under her breath. She prayed fervently that he would open his mouth and end the torture between them.

Instead of him answering with his voice, she heard his feet stepping gently in the water, the sucking, slapping, sloshing sound as he made his way past her body, out into the corridor, back into the bedroom. He still had not said a word, had not even bothered to turn off the tap. He had come in, looked, and walked out as though she had ceased to exist.

Certainly, this woman sprawled on the bathroom floor was totally different from the girl who had won a university scholarship, who had risen from a lowly field assistant to a managerial position. This could not be that intelligent girl, that ambitious girl full of confidence and life, full of dreams. That girl had been a fighter, not one who curls into her shell and waits for death. That girl would have simply packed her bags and walked away, started afresh, grown stronger from the betrayal. So who was this girl who was dying of hunger?

Love had turned a strong woman into a coward, thrown her into hopelessness. She turned her face into the jet of water gushing out of the tap, placed her mouth and nose right in the stream. The vision of a feast with her grandmother resurfaced with such vividness that the water became food. She could smell the aroma of the dishes spread on the table as the water rushed into her nose and filled her lungs.

She knew she was dead when she woke up under a river. Her grandmother was queen of the water kingdom, perched on a mighty throne of gold. Thousands of people were seated at the table as long as the river. She could not see the other end of it. Each guest had brought a pot of food to share. One man brought live frogs, they were fat and they hopped onto the plates, happy to be eaten. He said that his pot had broken at the doorway of the river, so he had to improvise. He spoke without opening his mouth. She could feel his words, as though they were solid living creatures coming to her in a dream. She tried to remember where her pot was, what had happened to it, why she had not brought any food to the feast. She thought her grandmother would expel her from the table, and so she opened her mouth to explain. No words came out.

Nothing but bubbles. She could not speak. Yet they understood without the need for speech that her pot had broken just after she had walked through the door, and so she had not had a chance to improvise the way this man had done with the frogs. The queen waved away her unspoken apology and pointed at the fat, green creature on her plate. It stared at her with large eyes, as the queen urged her to bite off its juicy legs. The warts on its skin made her retch. All the food she had already stuffed into her stomach came gushing up her throat and spewed out of her mouth and nose.

When she opened her eyes, she was on a bed, but not the bed in her marital home. Not the bridal bed in which she had lain starving for three days. This one felt small. It had no blankets. The sheets were green. Above her was a plastic bag attached to a long metallic pole. Liquid from the bag dripped into a tube attached to her arm. She could not understand what was going on until an old man in a white robe came to her, a strange instrument dangling on his chest. A doctor?

The doctor said something. She shook her head to indicate that she did not understand what he was saying, that he had to communicate the way dead people did. He nodded, but when he spoke again she could still not understand him. He gave her sweet syrup. The taste reminded her of the emptiness in her tummy. She licked the plastic spoon ravenously.

Later her husband came, hiding his hands behind his back. He brought with him a strong, pleasant smell that made her stomach grumble. What was he hiding? Akeyo? Biringanya? Roast beef? They stared into each other's eyes. In his eyes she saw that he loved her and, in spite of what had happened, she found she still wanted to be his wife. He smiled and revealed what had been hidden behind his back.

It was a rose. Her hands trembled as she took the flower. She could not hide her disappointment. A tear rolled down her cheek. He wiped it away. His finger was warm.

His lips moved. Strange sounds came out of his mouth. She hoped that he was explaining the photo, telling her that the woman was a con artist who had accused five other men of fathering the same baby. She hoped he was saying how much he loved her. She pressed her finger to his lips, shutting him up. She pointed into her mouth, made a chewing motion. He smiled, and hurriedly left the room. She stared at the door long after he had gone, wondering if he had understood, if he would bring her kwon kaal and smoked fish in groundnut sauce. If he would ever bring her what she wanted.

Dilman Dila is a Ugandan writer, film maker and a social activist who believes that stories are an important tool in creating a better world. He was shortlisted for the prestigious Commonwealth Short Story Prize 2013 and nominated for the 2008 Million Writers Awards for his short story, "Homecoming". He first appeared in print in The Sunday Vision *in 2001. His works have since featured in several zines and book anthologies, including the African Roar, Storymoja, and Gowanus books. His first novella,* Cranes Crest at Sunset, *was released during the Storymoja Hay Festival 2013. As a self-taught film maker, he has made a number of films, including* What Happened in Room 13 *(available on YouTube). His first narrative feature,* The Felistas Fable (2013) *is currently making the rounds in festivals. He keeps an online journal of his work and life at http://www.dilmandila.com.*

Heaven Scent

Katherine Graham

Marmalade rubbed herself against Ncumisa's leg as she fumbled to unlock the door. Clare was out, probably at the gym. Once more the thought occurred to Ncumisa, even more so now that the house was unoccupied: *This place is so empty*. It was immaculately clean as usual, the wooden floors gleaming, the scarlet scatter cushions perfectly arranged on the solemn black leather couches. Soulless. It looked more like a doctor's waiting room than a lounge.

Ncumisa switched the kettle on and rummaged through the fridge. On the first day she had worked there, Clare had nonchalantly swept her arm towards the kitchen. "Help yourself to anything you want," she had said. But there was nothing to eat, certainly nothing that was appetising. There was rye bread, which tasted off; tofu, which had no flavour at all; some milk for making tea at least; that was it. Ncumisa resolved there and then to bring her own food from home or to buy a vetkoek from the taxi rank, otherwise she felt sure she would starve.

She heard a plaintive cry and looked down; it was Marmalade. The poor cat was as hungry as she was. She filled her bowl with kibbles and returned to making her tea. A delicious smell crept through the window, filling her nostrils with the appealing promise of good food. Hearth food, home-cooked and wholesome, vegetables, spices, tomato broth and... what was it? Lamb, yes, lamb. It smelled like her mother's Transkei cooking, out on an open fireplace in a potjie.

Her reverie was shattered by the sound of keys jangling in the front door. Clare was home, dressed in her sports clothes. She had the most impossibly tiny bottom, Ncumisa marvelled. How white women could have such a small posterior was a mystery to her, she who had had an hour-glass figure from the age of 13. Clare's husband, Nick, had commented that his wife "had a body to die for", but Ncumisa wasn't so sure. It seemed to her that something was missing from her svelte frame, something soft and warm and feminine.

"There is the most beautiful smell coming from next door," said Ncumisa as Clare sipped a glass of water.

"Really?" replied Clare, betraying a hint of curiosity. "That's funny, I thought the house was empty."

In the semi-detached house alongside theirs lived a retired German couple that were swallows. They chased the summer sun like migrating birds, spending spring and summer in Cape Town, before returning to enjoy the same sequence of warm seasons in Berlin. They had been gone a month now, although Greta had said that an estate agent had been appointed to lease the house in their absence.

"Maybe you should go around and say hello?" suggested Ncumisa.

Clare smiled. *Yes*, she thought. *Perhaps I will.*

Juanita had the most enormous mane of hair that Clare had ever seen. It stuck up all around her round face, fuzzy and utterly untameable. Perched on her nose, which featured a gold ring, were a pair of black-rimmed glasses, which tempered the wild appearance of her hair. She clattered through the house with her high heels, bracelets and ankle chains all jingling in unison.

"Yes," she said. "We moved in two nights ago. We've just sold our flat in Woodstock and are staying here for a few months while we wait for our new house to be ready."

The first reason that prompted the move walked into the hallway. Noah looked about three, mucus stains streaked across his cheeks. A green slug peeked from his left nostril. He had the same Afro as his mother, only his was darker. He glared at Clare, kicked off his boots and darted back into his room.

"He was getting too big to live in a flat anymore," sighed Juanita. "There was no garden. Otherwise we could quite happily have stayed there."

The second reason was her ailing mother, whom Juanita referred to as Ma. Ma was the alchemist responsible for the intoxicating smells emanating from the kitchen. She was a tiny woman, hunched over the stove top, rendered almost invisible by the jets of steam coming from the collection of pots. She at least, Clare was pleased to note, did not have a huge head of hair. She had almost none, just a few strands scraped back into a bun.

"What are you making?" inquired Clare politely.

Ma cocked her head. Clare repeated her question.

"It's a bredie," she said. "You know what a bredie is?"

Clare shook her head.

"It's a stew. You fry the onion and the lamb and wait till it's braised. Then you add the stock and water with the carrots, the beans, the potatoes and the diced tomatoes. You see? It's easy. Then you gooi in the coriander right at the end. Fantasties!"

Juanita looked at her mother admiringly. "Ma is the only person I know who starts cooking supper at 11 o' clock in the morning," she said.

"Of course, of course," chuckled Ma. "Otherwise it just wouldn't taste right."

"Why don't you join us for supper tonight?" asked Juanita as she picked up Noah's boots.

"Oh, I..." Clare struggled for an excuse that wouldn't offend. "We don't want to impose."

"Nonsense! What time do you normally eat – 8 o' clock? Noah should be asleep by then. Bring a bottle of wine. We'll provide everything else."

"Well, I suppose..." Clare pushed back a few stray blonde hairs from her face. "We don't have anything else on. Thanks."

Two candles stood like sentries, guarding either end of the table, which had been draped with a Congolese cloth which glittered with bright geometric patterns. The food had already been placed in serving dishes, the smell of saffron rice rising delicately above the heady smell of red meat. "Wow," gasped Nick. "This looks like a feast."

He had been delighted when Clare told him about the invitation. Although theirs was a happy union, he often despaired over his wife's complete lack of cooking skills. Rather than upset her by complaining, he had opted for the path of least resistance: having a full-course meal at the office canteen and then eating soup and egg on toast in the evening. It was healthier to have a light meal at dinner time, he had reassured himself. And Clare seemed happy eating her steamed fish and anaemic vegetables, so they had reached an uneasy culinary compromise.

Ma, flushed with her efforts, collapsed down in a chair. Colin, Juanita's thick-set husband, sat at the head of the table and said grace. Nick couldn't make out what he said because it was in Afrikaans. He did catch one word – dankbaar. And that was how he felt – thankful.

They tucked into the meal and as the food slid down into their bellies, mixing with the full-bodied Merlot, they slowly attained that wonderful feeling of satiety, where your body feels heavy but your heart feels light. The conversation continued around them. Nick was explaining why his profession, architecture, was so subject to the whims of the economy, and Colin, a building contractor whose paint-stained hands attested to his work, agreed. "But there will always be work for us," he said, "because people like fixing up their houses. It's become a kind of national pastime. And rather spend a few thousand renovating your house than buy a new one, don't you think?"

Juanita smiled broadly at her husband. *She has the most perfect teeth*, mused Clare, who was always self-conscious of her own slightly skew ones. Juanita was a librarian, though since Noah had been born she had decided to stop working.

"And what do you do?" she asked, flashing her brilliant smile at Clare.

"I'm studying. Psychology. Part-time." The words shot out of her mouth at irregular intervals like bullets.

"Clare's a fitness instructor," said Nick. "That's why she has such an amazing body."

Clare fiddled with her wedding ring while her husband patted her shoulder affectionately – or condescendingly – Clare couldn't make out which.

"Oh," said Juanita, whose voluptuous figure was barely restrained in the floral dress she wore. "That's probably just what I need. I'd love to shed my baby weight."

"Well, Clare could use some cooking lessons, so maybe you can help each other out. What do you say, babe?"

Clare smiled thinly. She couldn't shake Nick's patronising tone. "Sure," she said. "Good idea."

"I'm absolutely famished!" Juanita clutched her belly for mock effect. "Surely after all that working out we can reward ourselves with a little snack?"

"Sure," said Clare, not wanting to sound like a spoilsport. "What did you have in mind?"

Juanita popped her head into the fridge. "Oh," she said flatly. "Not much here. Why don't you come over to my place?"

A sticky-sweet smell embraced them as they walked into Ma's kitchen. "Koeksisters," she said by way of greeting.

"Koeksisters? That's not very healthy," lamented Clare.

"But oh-so-utterly divine," countered Juanita, "especially my mother's."

Ma explained to Clare how they were made and the difference between the Afrikaans koeksisters – plaited and twisted – and the Malay ones, which were oblong in shape, laced with spices like ginger, cinnamon, aniseed and cardimom and then finely dusted with coconut.

"I could eat a dozen of them in one go," sighed Juanita.

"But you mustn't," chided Clare. "Remember your hard workout this morning. You don't want to undo it all."

Juanita's expression was sheepish. "We'll just have one or two."

Noah bounded down the passage, a bright look on his face. "Koeksisters! Yummy to tummy!"

Ma bent down and handed him one.

"Ma, Ma – put it on a plate, please." It was evident that Juanita was at pains to impress her visitor. "Sit down, Clare – we'll have tea in the lounge."

The lounge was an odd assortment of different-sized couches, all covered with the same Congolese fabric to conceal a multitude of sins – stains, tears and scuffs. Clare had the same feeling she might have had from sitting on a bus seat, the sickening thought of how many other people's bottoms had rested there before her, and their varying degrees of hygiene. She doubted whether Juanita ever bothered to clean her couches. The throws were just an attempt to disguise the real state of them. Gingerly, she eased herself onto the edge of the nicest-looking sofa.

Suddenly an oblique shaft of light illuminated her, bursting through the steely-grey clouds. Clare noticed the intense colours of the cloth and the intricate pattern of the design. All at once, the ritual of drinking tea overcame her, the poise of holding a cup on a saucer, the steam tickling her nose. She watched Juanita, deep at work dunking her koeksister in her cup, and decided to do the same. Sucking the tea through the gooey flesh of the doughnut was an oddly satisfying sensation. The coconut prickled her lips.

"We have a potluck club," Juanita interrupted her abstraction.

"What's a potluck club?" Clare dusted the crumbs off her mouth.

"Well, it's a bit like a stokvel. You know what that is, right?"

"Everyone pools their money together and then they each take turns at helping themselves to the cash."

"Basically, yes," said Juanita, slurping her tea and smacking her lips. "It's a club. We get together once a month. Everyone brings something that they've made. We eat and that's it."

"Sounds like fun." *Or not so fun*, thought Clare, *especially if it involves cooking or baking*.

"Would you like to join ours?" Juanita's pearly whites were catching the sunlight and dazzling her. "Or you could just come one night and give it a try?"

"Maybe," said Clare. "Okay."

The table was heaving with food, crowding out any attempt at decoration. Bobotie, sosaties, saffron rice with sultanas, rotis stuffed to overflowing with chicken curry and a vast array of side dishes, some of which Clare battled to identify. But it did look good, very good, and of course Nick hadn't hesitated when she'd asked him to accompany her.

"This is fit for a king," he declared.

Juanita bustled about the table, directing her guests where to sit. There was barely any elbow room; they all squashed together side by side and made small talk while the ocean of fragrances arising from the food washed over them.

"The bobotie I made," boasted a skinny woman with the word 'Beloved' tattooed on the inside of her forearm. "My mother taught me how to make it. The bay leaves give it its special flavour, but the egg custard on top is the bit that I like the best."

Clare nodded. She had no idea how to even attempt to make something as complicated as that. The only domestic instruction her mother had ever given her was how to put a clean duvet cover on without getting it all tangled up inside. All the cooking had been done by their cherished domestic worker, Zandile, or they had eaten convenience meals.

She watched Nick tuck into the food. He was chatting animatedly to Colin and gulping down mouthfuls between sips of red wine. She was reminded of how handsome he was, his distinguished jaw offsetting his slightly thinning dark hair. And suddenly it struck her – a sharp stab in her chest. *I've been depriving him of home-cooked food*, she thought. *All these years. What do they say about the way to a man's heart?*

After supper, as the guests milled around in the hallway, Clare resolved to tell Juanita. "I'll do it," she said.

"Do what?" Juanita's cheeks looked rosy and plump. Clare thought again how inviting her features were, even though they were slightly exaggerated. It was as if her face and body were bursting with life, like a ripe fruit hanging heavily from a tree.

"I'll join your potluck club. If you'll have me, that is. I'm no chef."

"Of course!" Juanita drew her closer, planting a kiss on her cheek. "You are most welcome. We'll make a good housewife out of you yet!"

The cake turned out flatter than Clare had hoped. The recipe didn't call for icing, but scrutinising it now, she wished she had bought that cream cheese after all. Ncumisa eyed her creation suspiciously.

"What is it?" she asked.

"It's a plum cake. A torte, actually."

Ncumisa looked baffled. "Aren't you meant to ice a cake?"

"Apparently not. Not this one."

"It seems a bit naked and upside-down."

"Yes, I suppose it does." *Oh, what on earth am I doing*, she groaned inwardly. *I should have just bought one of those boxes which has all the ingredients in it, where you just add two eggs, water and some oil. Then I couldn't have gone wrong. But instead I have to experiment with something exotic.*

"Put some cream on top," suggested Ncumisa, picking up the mop again. "I think I saw some in the fridge."

"What did you say it is?" The skinny tattooed woman pointed at the dense grey mass as the dollop of cream started oozing over the sides.

"It's a torte," Clare said confidently, although under the table her left foot flicked up and down with irritation.

"Oh," the woman replied. She patted her stomach. "I'll save some space for later."

You needn't bother, Clare seethed. But she consoled herself that she had found a harbour of comfort in her friendship with Juanita, who always seemed pleased when she dropped by or invited her to go to the gym. *She is so uncomplicated*, mused Clare, *compared to my other friends. With them, everything is carefully arranged and regulated. I'm allowed to see them at certain times, but not at others. With Juanita, I can pop around at any time and she's never offended or unwelcoming. Her hospitality is astounding*, she thought. It was a rare gift indeed. Her guests basked in her glow.

The torte was tentatively received. Everyone had a bite or two, which was more than Clare had expected. She got to take the rest home.

"Not bad, babes," was Nick's attempt at encouraging her. "Better luck next time, hey?"

But there was to be no next time. A few days' later, Clare had rung the neighbour's buzzer and heard no reply. *That's odd,* she thought. She walked the ten paces back to her front gate and noticed something sticking out of the letterbox – an envelope addressed to her. Intuitively, she knew what it contained. She thrust it under her arm and sighed, a deep exhalation, depleting her of something she realised was hope. *Six months. I should have known*, she thought. *I should have prepared myself for this.*

"They're gone," were the first words she said to Nick when he returned home that evening.

"Who? Gone where?"

"Juanita and Colin. They've moved into their new house. No more nice cooking. No more potluck club." The words were tipped in lead, sinking down through her navel and plopping onto the floor.

"Oh." Nick placed his hand gently on her bare shoulder and bent down to brush his lips on her skin.

"It doesn't have to be, honey." His words, light and silky, floated up to the ceiling where they lingered a while before fading. "It doesn't have to be the end."

The expression on Clare's face was fixed, one of dogged optimism, like a Staffordshire bull terrier tugging on a bone. This will be a success, she told herself. The hum of animated conversation buzzed around her as she fiddled with knobs and adjusted the timer. She took a glug of chenin blanc, then announced: "Supper will be served in five minutes."

Nick ushered the guests to their seats. He had brought home a bunch of yellow roses – her favourite – which went perfectly with the new African batik tablecloth she'd bought at Greenmarket Square. She gazed intently at the oven. Bubbles were pushing up to the surface excitedly. It was as if the casserole dish were begging her to be released.

Clare soaked up the chorus of approval as she placed the steaming dish on the table. The fronds of steam wove around them, infusing them with a tantalising medley of aromas.

"What is it?" her friend Stacey enquired.

"Bobotie," she beamed. "My first attempt. I hope it's good."

The jury was unanimous: a resounding success. "A triumph," Stacey had called it. Clare wafted on a cloud of contentedness as she refilled her guests' glasses.

"Where's the cat's mince?" called Nick from the kitchen. Marmalade was wrapped around his leg, meowing softly. "I could have sworn I left it on the counter to defrost."

The conversation turned to politics as Clare resumed her seat. They were talking about whether the ANC would win the next election, or rather, by how much. Which provinces they were likely to lose was a hot topic. Clare pushed her food around her plate, following the conversation with half an ear.

As the guests trickled out the door, she felt the comforting crook of Nick's arm around her waist. Stacey was the last to leave. "I'm super impressed," she enthused. "The food was amazing. Well done!"

"Beginner's luck," Clare smiled. She felt Nick squeezing her arm.

The door clicked shut. His knowing eyes met hers. "Cat got your tongue?" he asked.

Katherine Graham is a wordsmith by profession, who fills her days writing articles and looking after her two boys, husband and ginger cat. She studied at Rhodes University and worked for three years as an economics reporter at the SABC before doing a gap year in the UK. After a brief stint as a primary school teacher in Cape Town, she returned to writing and has remained in the world of media ever since, contributing travel, business and health articles to a number of magazines and newspapers. Creative writing is the next logical progression in her career and she is brooding over a number of projects at the moment, including a children's book, a play and a romantic historical novel. Katherine wants her work to be clearly situated in a South African context with all its nuances, not just the stereotypes that Hollywood projects.

The Dibbuk

Manu Herbstein

"In the years when we were afflicted with drought, they drank their fill; and in our years of famine, they feasted."

We buried Second Oubaas today. Or rather, they buried him.

It was a last-minute thought to take me with them to the cemetery. The coffin was already in the hearse and they were getting into the black Mercedes when Master Henry turned round and I heard him ask, "Where's Janet?"

I was standing at the top of the steps by the front door, in my apron, watching.

"Janet," Master Henry called, "Aren't you coming?"

He walked across to the Honda. It was already full, two in the front, three at the back.

"You'll just have to sit on Janet's lap," I heard him tell Naomi.

He beckoned with his hand. I showed him my apron and pointed to my bare head. He nodded and told them to wait for me.

On the way out, I paused in front of the hall mirror to put on my doek. Then Richard was chasing them through the traffic. Madam didn't come. She says funerals make her feel queasy.

At the Pinelands cemetery, I stood to one side, reading the writing on the slabs while the Rabbi chanted away and they responded.

I know that Rabbi. When he comes to the house, he shakes my hand and remembers my name. He has a friendly smile but his teeth are not too good.

All the tombstones have a cross of David on them. The writing is neat, in Hebrew and English, cut into the polished black marble.

Our cemeteries are not so tidy. Overgrown, more likely. We respect our dead but who has the money to pay for weeding and cutting the grass? If you ask the City Council, they say they are broke. But they're not so broke when it comes to the white cemeteries.

"The City Council? Cut the grass? That'll be the day," Rosa says.

Rosa is my granddaughter. She's a student at the University of the Western Cape. She's clever. She had an offer to go to UCT but she turned it down.

They finished their prayers. Master Henry sent Naomi to ask me if I'd like to throw some soil on the coffin. I said no thank you, but Naomi insisted. She took my hand and led me to the grave. The mourners moved to one side to let us through. Master Henry handed me a spadeful of earth.

"Say goodbye to your friend, Janet," he said.

It was Master Henry's uncle he was talking about, his father's brother.

I turned the spade to let the soil trickle onto the box, gently, not to make too much noise, not to wake the dead.

"Thank you, Master Henry," I said.

"We were lucky to get a place for him next to my father. Twin brothers who never knew one another."

He shook his head as if he still didn't believe it.

"Have you seen my father's headstone?" he asked. "No, you couldn't have. You didn't come to the consecration, did you?"

It said, "In loving memory of Arnold Levy, passed away . . . aged 80 years. Deeply mourned by his devoted daughter, son, daughter-in-law, grandchildren and great-grandchildren."

The daughter lives in Israel. As for the daughter-in-law, she never had any time for the Oubaas. I was the one who had to nurse him. She never lifted a finger.

The others were walking down to the gate to wash their hands.

"Well, I'm glad that's over," Master Henry said. "And I'm sure that you are too, Janet."

That's how they are. He thinks he can look into my mind, like through a window, and see what's inside.

Every year they celebrate the Passover. In the old days, it was the Oubaas, Arnold Levy, Master Henry's father, who sat in the big armchair at the head of the table, yarmulke on his bald head, white and blue prayer shawl around his shoulders. Sometimes there would be twenty of them, family and guests. I would have to slide the top of the stinkwood dining table open and put in two extra boards to make room for them all. Even then, there were sometimes too many and I had to set another table for the children.

While the Oubaas was reading the story of the Jews' escape from slavery in a language none of them understood, I would be in the kitchen, warming the plates and making sure the chicken soup and matzo balls and the gefilte fish would be ready when Madam called.

By that time old Mrs Levy had died and the Oubaas had moved in with us. As he got older, I had to be his nurse. He wouldn't let Master Henry's wife touch him. But with me, he could even crack a joke when I gave him a bed-bath. He had grown up in the platteland where his father had a shop. He liked to talk to me in Afrikaans but I always answered him in English.

Once he showed me a black and white photograph in an old album. The name of the business was painted in big letters stretching across the front of the building: SAMUEL LEVY, ALGEMENE HANDELAAR.

"Samuel Levy was my father," he said. "He was born in the old country. A genuine Litvak."

"That's me," he said, pointing to a boy in short pants standing in front of the shop.

And so he would go on.

When the Oubaas died, I thought he might have left me something in his will to say thank you for the care I gave him in his old age. But either he forgot, or maybe he just had nothing left. I don't really know.

One thing I forgot to say. The year Nelson Mandela was released, that was 1990, they decided that I should sit at the table with them. Not for every meal, of course, just for the Seder, the Passover meal. The Oubaas made a speech, linking Mister Mandela's release to the Israelites' delivery from slavery in Egypt and he said it had always been their custom to keep a spare seat ready for any poor person who happened to be passing. So from then on, I sat with them on Seder night, at the bottom end of the table, near the kitchen.

When I told Rosa this story, she laughed that nasty laugh of hers.

"And who was sitting in that chair all through the years of apartheid?" she asked.

"Hai, Miss Clever," I told her. "What do you know about apartheid? You weren't even born then."

"Gran," she said. "Don't you know? Apartheid is still with us."

I can't argue with the girl. She is too clever for me.

When Rosa was in her matric year, they invited her for the Seder and since then they expect her to come every year. At first I know she enjoyed it, she told me so, but once she started at the University her views began to change.

"We are just their window-dressing," she says. "It makes them feel good that we are there. It lets them bluff themselves that they never benefitted from apartheid."

Ag, Rosa. I don't know what will become of her. Maybe if she gets married, that will cure her sickness.

Anyway, the last Seder, Rosa was there, sitting by my side.

I had warned her, "No politics tonight, hear?"

Once she got into an argument with Richard. She said, "The Zionists are treating the Palestinians just like the Boers treated us people." He called her an anti-Semite. She called him a racist. It was ugly. That's why I warned her: no politics.

It is the job of the youngest boy to ask the four questions which set off the annual story telling. The questions start like this: Mah Nishtanah Halayilah Hazeh, which means, "What makes this night different from all other nights?" Because the questions are in some old dead language which nobody speaks any more, the small boy has to learn them off by heart. I know them off by heart myself because I have been rehearsing them with small boys in this family since I was a young girl. Even before I started working for them, when my mother was working here and I was still at school, I rehearsed them. The first was Master Henry himself. But this year all the nephews and grandsons and great-grandsons had been taken to Israel for the Passover and so the task fell to Naomi.

Everything went on as usual. Master Henry read the story, the answer to the four questions, from the picture book they call the Hagadah. The Oubaas used to read it in Hebrew, which no one understood, and so it was boring. Since the

Oubaas passed away, Master Henry has read it in English. Most of it is still quite boring so I'm not going to repeat it here.

Near the end, Master Henry called Naomi to watch as he poured red wine into a glass.

Just then, there was a buzz from the intercom at the front gate. Master Henry showed me with a nod of his head that I should answer it.

"Is this Mr. Henry Levy's house?" the voice said.

It was a coloured voice.

"Can I speak with Mr. Levy, please?"

"I'm sorry," I said, "Mr. Levy is not available right now. Please try again some other time," and pressed the off button.

Master Henry nodded to show me I had done the right thing.

"Naomi," he said then, "do you see this glass of red wine? It is for Elijah the Prophet. Now I want you to go to the front door and open it. Open it just a little. Be careful not to remove the chain, mind. Then hold the door open to let Elijah come in and take a sip of wine from the glass. Keep the door open to let him go out. Then, when I call you, you can close the door behind him. Can you do it? Can you reach the handle?"

Naomi gave a vigorous nod; and off she went.

Master Henry raised Elijah's glass. There were smiles all round. Every year the same performance. But this year it was different. This night really was different from all other nights.

Master Henry still had Elijah's glass at his lips when Naomi came running back, so excited that she didn't see the fraud.

"Grandpa, Grandpa," she called. "Zeider's standing outside the door. He wants to come in, but I can't lift the chain."

Zeider means grandfather in Yiddish. That's what Naomi used to call the Oubaas, her great-grandfather, Arnold Levy, who had died three months before.

"What can have got into the child's head?" Master Henry said. "Here, Naomi, see the wine glass. It's half-full. Elijah came in and drank some while you were at the door."

But Naomi had lost interest in Elijah the Prophet.

She insisted, "Grandpa, Zeider Arnold's standing outside. Won't you come and let him in?"

Master Henry raised his voice above the buzz of puzzled talk at the table.

"Ruthie," he said to Naomi's older sister. "Won't you go and see what this is all about? But don't on any account remove the security chain. Do you understand?"

When she came back into the dining room just a few seconds later, Ruth's face was paler than I've ever seen it.

"Grandpa," she said, her voice scarcely above a whisper, "it's true. Zeider's standing outside the door. And there's a man, a coloured man, standing at the gate, with a taxi in the road behind him. When he saw me, he said, 'Won't you let the old man in, little girl?'"

Master Henry bit his lip. His face was stern. I guess he suspected that this was some sort of family conspiracy to make a fool of him, a Passover practical joke perhaps.

"This is Tuesday," he said. "April Fool's Day is on Thursday, the day after tomorrow. Now what the hell is going on here? Richard, please go and sort this out."

Richard is Ruth and Naomi's father, Master Henry's only son. Master Henry doesn't think much of him. I've heard him refer to Richard as a nincompoop.

"Dad," said Richard, when he came back from his trip to the front door, "I think you'd better come."

Master Henry stood up with a scowl that seemed to reveal his contempt for the whole human race, including his own family.

In the hush, we heard the sound of the chain being unlatched and the creak of the hinges on the door.

"Good evening. Chag sameach. Happy holiday," we heard Master Henry say.

Then, "Richard. Quick. See if you can catch the taxi."

But the taxi driver had done his job and driven off. Richard didn't get his number.

Master Henry led an old man into the dining room. It was the Oubaas, or if it wasn't him, it was his ghost. Or his double, or whatever. I screamed, but my scream was drowned by Madam's. Her scream was so loud it must have carried all the way from Green Point to Adderley Street. I'm surprised the neighbours didn't report it to the police.

Rosa said, "The spitting image."

I recovered quickly and went to help Madam. Master Henry tried to get her to sip a tablespoon of brandy. Meanwhile the old man just stood there, clutching a cardboard carton to his chest, with a bemused expression on his face.

"Janet," said Master Henry, "take her to her bedroom, and give her a tranquilizer and a sleeping pill."

When I got back to the dining room, they had taken his cardboard box from the old man and sat him down on the chair on Master Henry's right. Master Henry was sprawled out on his armchair, his eyes closed, biting his lower lip and nodding his head slowly, pausing, and then nodding it again. Naomi said, "Grandpa, is he Elijah?"

"Ja," said Master Henry, "Elijah the Prophet, taking potluck at our seder."

Richard had taken the chair opposite the old man and was talking to him.

"Old man, can you understand me?" No response. "Old man, can't you hear me?" Again, no response, except to look at Richard with a sweet smile.

"He must be deaf and dumb," Richard said.

Master Henry opened his eyes and sat up.

"Rubbish," he said. "Can't you see? He's an idiot."

"Grandpa!" Ruth objected.

"An idiot," Master Henry repeated. "I use the word, my dear Ruthie, in its precise, scientific meaning. He has the mental capacity of a two-year-old. Or less. Brain damaged at birth. You're wasting your time trying to communicate with him."

"Oy vey!" said old Mrs Cohen from next door.

"You're joking," said Richard's wife, Sarah.

"How do you know?" Richard asked.

"But who is he?" Rosa wanted to know.

They all spoke at once. Master Henry ignored them.

"Janet," he said to me, "Let's have some food, shall we?"

As I came back to the dining room with the tureen with the chicken soup and matzo balls, I heard Mrs Cohen telling Rosa, "A dibbuk. I'm convinced of it. He's a dibbuk. Or should I say it's a dibbuk."

Sarah sent the first bowl of soup to the old man.

"A dibbuk, Mrs Cohen? What's a dibbuk?" Rosa asked.

"A dibbuk," Mrs Cohen replied, "is an evil spirit. Like your tokolosh."

Mrs Cohen came to South Africa after the war. She has a number tattooed on her right forearm. Her English is funny. And she can't tell the difference between blacks and coloureds.

Master Henry caught my eye and pointed. Then he did a bit of mime with a soupspoon. I went and stood behind the old man and fed him, spoon by spoon. He dribbled, so I tied a serviette around his neck. He didn't object, just drank the soup. He was well behaved. All the time he stayed with us, Second Oubaas was well behaved. Within his capacity, of course.

"Why do you think he's a dibbuk?" Rosa asked Mrs Cohen.

"Tell me," said Mrs Cohen, "isn't he the spitting image of old Arnold? Isn't he?"

Rosa had to agree. She had used those very same words.

"Well, the Arnold I knew, Henry's father, Richard's grandfather, Ruth and Naomi's great-grandfather, was a good man. I have no doubt about that. At least all the years I knew him. And we are told not to speak ill of the dead, so I hope Arnold, wherever he is, will forgive me. But some time in his youth, he must have committed a terrible sin. And God is punishing him. He won't let Arnold's spirit rest in peace. He has sent it back into the world of the living in this . . . this dibbuk."

I had finished feeding Second Oubaas his soup and the rest of them had finished theirs too, so I collected the bowls and took them to the kitchen. Rosa followed with the empty tureen.

"What about you, Gran?" Rosa asked me.

"After," I said. "Now please take the gefilte fish in and I'll bring the plates from the warming oven."

Mrs Cohen was sulking, so I guess that Master Henry must have had some words with her while we were out of the room. Master Henry doesn't suffer fools gladly, like St. Paul said in his second letter to the Corinthians. I have heard Master Henry call Mrs Cohen an old fool. Behind her back, of course.

Next was the roast chicken and roast potatoes; and then the trifle and the ice cream. I was tired. I had been cooking the whole day. After I'd served the men their coffee, it was time for the girls to hunt for the piece of matzo that Master Henry had hidden and which they would sell to him. While they did that, I thought I would sit at the kitchen table and have my own meal. But it was not to be.

"Janet," Master Henry called to me, "Is the bed in the guest suite made up?"

"Yes, sir," I told him.

I always keep that room ready in case of unexpected guests.

"Won't you please take this old man up there and put him to bed? You'd better help him to piss or he might wet the bed. And you'll probably have to undress him. Take a pair of my old pyjamas. You know where to find them."

A week ago, it was my birthday. On my day off Rosa came to fetch me in her old Beetle. We took the High Level Road into Buitengracht and then up to Kloof Nek and the Cable Station. I was born in the shadow of that mountain and all these years I had never been to the top. So this was Rosa's birthday present to me. I was a little nervous on the way up, hanging in mid-air like that, so first we went to the café to have a cup of tea and calm me down.

"How is Second Oubaas?" she asked me.

"Same as usual," I told her. "Sinking slowly. There's a day and a night nurse now. That takes a burden off my shoulders. Before he got sick, I had to bath him and dress him. It was hard work. But this is my day off. Let's talk about something else. Tell me about your studies."

"I can't tell you about my studies without talking about Mister Henry Levy and his uncle," she said.

"His uncle?" I asked.

"Ja," she said, "Second Oubaas is his uncle. His real name is Leslie Levy."

"How did you find that out? If you ask him, 'Old man, what is your name,' he just looks at you and smiles."

"Gran," she said, "to get my degree I have to do a research paper. They let me choose my own subject, so I settled on the Levy family, your Levy family."

"Now why would you do that?"

"Well, to start with, I was intrigued by Second Oubaas, Leslie Levy. That was such a strange evening, that Passover night when he turned up on their doorstep. I just couldn't get it out of my mind. But that was just the start. You won't believe all I've found out about them, particularly your Master Henry."

"I hope he won't hear about this," I said. "He won't like it at all."

"He'll hear about it, alright," she said, "I'm nearly ready to ask him for an interview. I'm just waiting for a few more documents from the Archives in Pretoria."

"What if he won't talk to you?"

"He'll talk. When he knows what I've found, he'll talk alright."

"Rosa," I said, "Why do you always look for trouble? He'll sack me. Sowaar."

"After you have worked for them for nearly fifty years? Just let him try," she said. "Times have changed, Gran. And he must know that. He wouldn't have a chance in the Labour Court. Come, if you've finished your tea, let's go for a walk."

When we had walked for a while, we sat down on a flat rock to watch the dassies. Rosa had brought a pair of binoculars. We looked at Robben Island and she promised to take me there. Then we talked.

"I remember you telling me," Rosa said, "that First Oubaas once showed you an old photograph album. Do you know where it is? Would it still be in their house? Do you think you could find it and let me borrow it for a few days, to scan the pictures?"

"I can't promise," I said, "but I'll look for it. But why?"

"Just interested," she said. "I'd like to see a picture of their father Samuel Levy and his wife. Leah she was called. Leah gave birth only once, to twins. Samuel planned to bring her to Cape Town for her confinement but the birth was premature and all he could do was to send to the coloured location for a birth attendant. Arnold arrived first but there was a problem with delivering the second boy, Leslie.

"The twins were identical, but it must have become clear quite soon that there was something wrong with Leslie. They brought them to Cape Town and the doctor here told them that the child's brain was damaged and he would never live a normal life. I guess they had some difficult decisions to make. In the end they sent him as far away as possible, to a home for the care of the mentally handicapped in Durban.

"I don't think they ever saw him again, but I guess they couldn't forget his existence. I've seen their will. They left half of their property to Arnold and the other half to a trust which they set up to provide for Leslie's care for the rest of his life."

"Did Oubaas know about this, do you think? He never said anything to me about it."

"I think he must have known, but the subject must have been taboo. Something shameful, not to be talked about. That's one reason I want to see the album. There might be pictures of the two babies in it. If there are, I guess that would tell us that he did know."

"What about Master Henry?" I asked. "I've tried once or twice to ask him about Second Oubaas but each time he shut me up."

"The taboo again. But don't you remember what he said at the Seder? 'The man's an idiot.' It just came out. It was a shock for him. He hadn't had time yet to decide how to deal with the situation.

"I found the annual reports of that home in the Social Welfare Department archives. They looked after Leslie until last year, nearly eighty years, how's that? Then the stock market crashed, if you remember, and the trust ran out of funds.

The home's income dried up and I guess they decided to disperse their remaining charges. I can't tell you how they found the Green Point address. I haven't managed to track them down. And I can't afford to go to Durban. Anyway, it's not important now."

"Rosa, my child," I said then, "Are they going to give you a degree for digging up this stuff? Does it matter?"

"Gran, Arnold and Leslie Levy are just a footnote. The one whose history is really interesting is your Master Henry Levy."

"Ag, man. What again?"

"Henry Levy is one of the richest men in the country. Certainly one of the top hundred."

"Is it now?" I asked.

"In the late seventies the Oubaas and his Afrikaner partner made a small fortune supplying the SADF for their war in Namibia and Angola."

"The Oubaas? I never knew. What did he supply?"

"Everything. Uniforms, tents, food. Whatever they needed. You name it. But mainly arms and ammunition. From Israel. And they were into diamonds and ivory too."

"Well I never. I remember that Henry fought in that war. There used to be a photograph of him in uniform hanging in the entrance hall, but after Mister Mandela was released he removed it to his study."

"When Henry was demobbed," Rosa said, "he joined his father in the business. Ten years later they were at it again. The supply contracts are in the archives. I've photocopied them all."

"And yet every time I ask him for a pay rise, he resists, offers me less. He says he gives me free accommodation, free electricity, free television, free medical; what do I need the money for, he asks me."

"Gran," Rosa said, "You might not know it but your Master Henry has a reputation for generosity; and it's true: I have the evidence. He's a philanthropist."

I was about to object but she held up her hand.

"Just guess where his donations go. I'll tell you. Most go to Israel. And practically all the rest to Jewish causes, schools, libraries, scholarships. It's all there on record."

"If you say that, they'll accuse you of anti-Semitism."

"Well, they'd be wrong. I judge people by what they do, not by what they are. Anti-Zionist, yes, but that is because of what the Israelis have done to the Palestinians, taking their land from them. But let's not go into that. It's your birthday. Look what I've brought."

It was a nice birthday cake, with seven candles and writing in pink icing, which said, 'Happy birthday, Gran.' Only, with the wind up there on the mountain, we had trouble lighting the candles.

We buried Second Oubaas today.

Now I'm going to talk to Master Henry about my retirement, my pension. Rosa has told me what to ask for: a lump sum, enough to buy and furnish a small flat; and my wages and medical insurance to continue for the rest of my life. She says I deserve it after working for them for half a century.

We buried Second Oubaas today.

Old Mrs Cohen said he was a dibbuk, some spirit of the past which comes back to haunt us.

Rosa says, "You can't bury the past."

She says we all have our dibbuks.

"Our own are the spirits of our San and Khoi and slave ancestors whom we denied for so long," she says.

"Every white South African has his black dibbuk," she says.

"And there's a Palestinian dibbuk for every Israeli, if not for every Jew."

That's what Rosa says.

Manu Herbstein was born in Muizenberg in 1936. He has lived in Ghana since 1970 and has dual South African and Ghanaian citizenship. He has written four novels and is working on a fifth. Ama, a Story of the Atlantic Slave Trade, won the 2002 Commonwealth Writers Prize for the Best First Book. Brave Music of a Distant Drum, *a sequel to* Ama, *was published in Canada in 2011.* Akosua and Osman *won a Burt Award for African Literature in Ghana in 2012.* Ramseyer's Ghost, *a political thriller set in Ghana in 2050, was long-listed in the 2013 Kwani Manuscript Project. He is currently working on an illustrated historical novel,* The Boy who Spat in Sargrenti's Eye. *Manu has had shorter work published in* African Writing, Baobab, Slavery and Abolition, Chimurenga, *the* African Cities Reader *and online. He is an active member of the Ghana Association of Writers.*

44 Boston Heights, Yeoville

Catherine Jarvis

I discovered the tin box the same day that I found the letter pinned to our front door and that all my savings had disappeared from my cupboard. Those three events are threaded together in my memory, and not only because they occurred on the same day.

Darkness had already settled when I returned home from work that day. My soles throbbed with every step I took up the stone staircase of Boston Heights. I counted on my prune fingers the number of hours I had been on my feet and I came to the ninth finger. The salon had overbooked and I had been washing hair and sweeping up curls of blonde, chestnut brown and auburn hair even through my thirty-minute lunch 'hour'.

I lurched up the unusually quiet steps of Boston Heights, clutching my bag which contained my day's wages. R100. Normally I would have to side-step teenagers splayed over the steps, their hands clasping brown bottles, but tonight the stairwell was empty except for a Doritos packet dancing back and forth on the top step.

I looked at the dilapidated building with a heavy heart. Ngwatilo told me that I was lucky to find this place. When she first arrived, she lived in a hijacked building and had to pay a drug lord rent every week.

As I approached the fourth floor, and the one-bedroom flat I shared with a Congolese family of four, I clutched my bag tightly to my belly, relieved that my R100 earnings had survived the trip home. My relief evaporated when I saw the notice on the door of our flat.

I didn't read it. I knew what it said.

I snatched it off the door, yanked it into the flat and placed it on the kitchen counter, where Maria was hunched over the stove. I heard the muffled giggles of the girls, Marie-Eve and Cecile, coming from the lounge, which the family used as a bedroom. It was separated from the kitchen by two sheets now dappled with cooking grease. I had the actual bedroom, which I sub-let from Maria and Joseph.

My bedroom door was not really a door. I had pinned one of my long black pashminas to the top of the door frame. The scarf wasn't quite long enough to cover the entire doorway, leaving about a foot open at the bottom. Marie-Eve and Cecile would poke their laughing faces through it, watch me, and ask me a thousand questions all at once.

I took out the money from my bag and counted it again and then took out my small notebook which my aunt had given to me as a going away present. It was a child's pocket-sized notebook with a grinning cartoon bear on the front, which always made me laugh as I used it for the serious purpose of keeping careful account of my money. I flipped through the pages, smiling as I surveyed the progress from page to page – my evening ritual. I had worked throughout the Christmas period and the clients – normally stingy – were feeling quite generous and gave me a few hefty tips.

I wrote "R100" next to the date: 14 January 2013. My savings were kept right at the back of the top shelf of the cupboard, wrapped in an ugly bright turquoise overall that no one would want to steal. Twice before, I had come home to find that one of my pretty T-shirts had been repossessed by somebody in the building.

I pulled the clothes down, trying to find the rough overall. It was always at the back and just within reach if I tip-toed on the bottom shelf. This time I couldn't grasp it. I started wrenching each item of clothing onto the floor. It simply was not there and, for an instant, I doubted whether it ever had been.

Besides the R100 I earned that day, that turquoise overall stored all the wealth I had in the world. Illegal immigrants don't get bank accounts. I immediately felt stupid for thinking I had been so clever to hide my money in an ugly item of clothing.

I lay on my mattress for a long time clutching the money I earned that day. My eyes were wide open, gaping at the drooping sepia pressed ceiling, with its patchy frame of black mould. I felt unable to move, unable to feel anything. When the noises in the flat softened to quiet murmurs and snores, I mustered up the energy to find a better hiding place.

I sat up and scanned the small, sparse room which had so few places to hide things. Then my eyes fell on the wooden floorboards. I drew my pen knife from my hoodie pocket and inspected the boards before lifting my sagging mattress and propping it against the window. I crouched to the ground and saw one plank slightly raised above its neighbours. I pressed it with my knee and it seemed to spring faintly. My knife slid easily into the grimy crevice between the boards and I heaved up this distinctive plank. It shifted and lifted up and finally loosened into my hands.

Clouds of dust and dirt lined the hollow beneath the board and I imagined hordes of rats housed there. Instead, I saw something glinting amidst the dirt. I carefully unearthed it and wiped the layer of dust from its surface. In my hands was a cold metal box, the shape and size of a lunchbox. When I picked it up, I could feel the contents shifting inside.

A flash of memory seared through me as I held it in my hand: of Mwende and me holding onto a box so similar in size and shape. Suddenly I could see Mwende's laughing eight-year-old face, her plump cheeks bulging.

I couldn't bear to hold that dusty tin box any longer. My hands shook as I bandaged it in a thin blue cotton scarf and stowed it at the back of the cupboard where my shoes lay. Then I stashed my notes – three gold and four green – in an old plastic bank bag, deposited it under the floor, and sealed the loose board back in its place beneath my mattress.

When I woke up the next morning, my mind lunged towards the box stashed away in my cupboard. This was someone's box. They had hidden it. They wanted to keep it a secret, buried within the building. Did I really want to see what someone had carefully kept hidden? Shame washed over me for piercing their privacy so casually. But shame felt better than grief.

My reverie was broken by Cecile's tiny head, crowned with little afro-puffs, poking under my pashmina-door, babbling breathlessly. I could barely understand what she was gabbing on about, but she mentioned 'yellow letter' several times and then I remembered: the notice on the door. Stumbling past a chattering Cecile, I headed to the kitchen where I heard Joseph and Maria speaking in hushed urgent tones. Joseph, wearing his faded olive-green uniform, nodded to me and growled rapidly in Congolese French to his wife. He put on his Tactical Security cap and slammed the door on his way out.

A sobbing Maria pressed the letter into my hand and gestured for me to read it.

> The CITY OF JOHANNESBURG has identified YEOVILLE as one
> of the areas to be included in our URBAN RENEWAL PROJECT.
> The building, BOSTON HEIGHTS, has been selected as one of
> FIFTY buildings that will be transformed from its current state
> into habitable, highly attractive homes. The CITY OF JOHAN-
> NESBURG has employed the eviction company REDEFINE to
> ensure a swift removal of all residents on 14 FEBRUARY 2013.
> We urge all residents to remove all personal belongings before this
> date.

It was dated November 2012 but they had only posted it on our door the previous day, giving us a month's notice. I didn't know what to say to Maria, who was looking at me, hopeful that I would be able to dispel any fears she had. Cecile appeared next to me, ready to translate the news.

Cecile did her best to translate what I had said, but I knew she didn't understand what I meant by 'government' and 'removal'. Maria shrugged helplessly when she was told the news, then said "au revoir" as she left for her cleaning job.

"What's this?"

I spun around to see Marie-Eve, her eyes opened wide, walking into the kitchen, holding the metallic box with great care as though it were a small coffin.

I snatched it from her hands. "This is private, Marie. You cannot go through my things."

Marie-Eve and Cecile watched as I marched back to my room. I decided that I couldn't leave the box there. If a little girl could find it, imagine the other people who wandered in with the intention to steal. So, I put it back where it belonged, beneath the floorboards and it remained unopened.

That evening the residents of Boston Heights held a meeting in the courtyard. I sat and listened as people spoke about the eviction notice. I did not really understand what they were saying but there seemed to be agreement that we would fight this. The knot of worry that had settled in my stomach the first time I had glimpsed the notice began to loosen.

When I came back from the meeting, the apartment was quiet. Even Cecile and Marie-Eve weren't there. In the distance, I heard someone starting up West African music and the smell of East African cuisine invaded the air around me. It was the way of life here; everywhere you turned there were people from all over Africa. You could see it by their skin tones, their flamboyant outfits, the foods they cooked, the jewellery they wore.

It was different at home. Not Nairobi. Turbi. I try not to think of the village too often as the memories still send razors to my heart. But when I saw Marie-Eve with the box in her hand, I saw Mwende. And Mwende exists in my memories of Turbi, where she will never leave.

I felt an urge to look through the box I had discovered. It became the box that Mwende and I had shared. Our box had been left in Turbi, also buried in our secret place. There had been no time to dig it out, even though I cried and pleaded with my aunt. She said there was no time and we left without the box. Without Mwende.

I moved quickly to my room and pulled open the loose floorboard and glared at the tin box. I held it in my hand. I thought about the memories hidden inside and wanted them to swallow up the memories of Turbi that were overpowering me.

The front door slammed open and I jumped in fright. I placed the box back and closed the floorboard quickly.

For the next two weeks, every time I entered Boston Heights, rumours about our eviction swirled around. People started locking the rusted security gate at the entrance in some feeble attempt to keep the eviction at bay. I noticed that the nice Ugandan family at number 15 had moved out one Sunday afternoon. Other residents spoke about leaving but most of us had nowhere else to go.

One day, while I placed my money in the plastic bank bag, I picked up the tin box again. I felt an urge to open it. Mwende would have opened it. She loved that we had a secret box that no one else in the village knew about. We never kept anything of value in it – there was no wealth in Turbi. But we would stash anything we found important or interesting in our box. When a friend at school had given me a red colouring pencil, I placed it in the box for Mwende and me to share. Mwende found a funny heart-shaped stone and placed it ceremoniously into our box. Bits of bright coloured material, a piece from a chess set – anything we thought was valuable to us – we hid in our box.

I looked at this tin box and wondered what someone else may have thought valuable enough to hide away from the world. I needed to know. I needed to stop thinking about Mwende. I opened the box and gasped at its contents – not chess pieces or coloured cloth, but photographs, a book and a diamond ring.

I picked up the ring first. The diamond was very simple in design and had dulled in colour, unpolished for years. I picked it up and placed it on my ring finger. It slipped on easily. I left it there as I looked through the photographs. A young white woman was in some of the pictures. She had dark hair that curved into a short bob and was young – like me – in her twenties. I turned over the first picture, which was of her sitting on a beach smiling shyly at the camera, and saw the number 1979 etched in pencil in looping feminine curves.

I recognised the location of the next picture. It was this flat; the Congolese family's bedroom – her living room, neat and complete with armchairs and a record player in the corner. She was standing next to a stiff-looking white man with dark hair, sharply slicked back. He did not smile, although she did, snuggled under his arm.

A series of photographs followed, which I viewed with disbelief. There was a black man in them and he was not the hired help. He was wearing a suit in every picture. It was the same suit in each picture, but still. The first was one with the white man and they were posing – shaking hands – as though they had just made some kind of deal. The white man looked awkward again but the black man had a beaming smile and looked at ease. Fascinated, I turned the picture over and saw

large loopy cursive writing announcing: *Partners! John Curtis and Mandla Sithole.*
I guessed it must have been a business deal of some sort.

The next few pictures were taken at a different time – it could have been
months or years later; there were no dates or captions written at the back of them,
as though they were not printed for anyone to see. It was summer and Mandla's
hairstyle was different, longer with a deep side path. He was sprawled on the
grass, big '70s sunglasses encasing his face and that same wide smile. The next
picture was taken at what looked like an office Christmas party. In the back-
ground, there were lots of white people dancing with Christmas hats on their
heads and one man had tinsel wound around his neck. In the foreground were
Mandla and the white lady. They were not sitting very close together; in my mind,
I imagined that they had deliberately sprung apart when the camera came to take
a snap. They both smiled at the camera, but I easily recognised that it wasn't one
of Mandla's real smiles and hers looked just as forced.

The very last picture was a shot of five people standing around our living
room, clutching glasses filled to the brim as though celebrating some occasion.
The lady was at the centre with John and he had his arm around her; for the first
time he was grinning and comfortable and she stood next to him with a demure
smile on her face. The rest of the guests were white, except for Mandla who held
his glass just slightly lower than everyone else's. He smiled comfortably at the
camera, but (I already felt like I knew him) he did not appear as jovial as the others.

The last item left in the box was a hardcover book. It was brown in colour
with no illustration: just the title and author's name. *The Hobbit* by J.R.R. Tolkien.
I opened the front cover and there was an inscription, written in small cursive
writing at the very top edge of the page: *Best – M.* I searched through the book
looking for more hidden clues but there were none. I wasn't even sure if it had
been read.

Once I had seen the items, I placed them all back in the box and stowed it under the floorboards along with my money. For the days that followed, I obsessed
over the items in the box. I invented stories about each of these people and they

became as real to me as Cecile and Marie-Eve. While I was at work I would look more carefully at the customers as I washed their hair, wondering if one of them was the mystery resident of 44 Boston Heights.

I invented so many different stories for them, particularly for the former resident, but they were always centred on a love triangle between her, John and Mandla. I decided her name was Sarah – just because – and she was the object of both John and Mandla's affections. It was always a classic love story set during apartheid. Sarah's true love was Mandla, but she could never be with him and instead settled unhappily with John.

The eviction date neared, and I saw more people bringing those big blue and white canvas Ghana-Must-Go bags into their apartments: people were packing up their lives. I decided to do the same. The night before the 14th of February, I packed up my all my clothes and the few items I had. I also took my money and the tin box and placed them in the bag, right at the bottom. I waited for Redefine, but they did not arrive. That night, the residents of Boston Heights were joyful.

There was a spontaneous party in the courtyard in the inner square of the flats. Everyone brought something. The Ethiopian family brought spongy injera flat bread with a stew so spicy it burned all the way from the back of your throat to your stomach. Nigerians brought jollof rice, chin-chin and fried plantains. The air was thick with smoke as the braai burned the countless cuts of meat. Crates of beer appeared and people passed quarts around to every person they saw. Neighbours who had previously bickered were now slapping each other on the backs and fist bumping. Cecile and Marie-Eve and dozens of other children danced around the courtyard in triumph, eyes shining with innocent excitement – not quite understanding the reason for the celebration, but infected by the festive atmosphere.

I stood aside from the noise with Anna who lived at number 12. She was Zimbabwean and Boston Heights had been her home for two years.

"It's the third eviction notice we've received here," she said, shrugging. "But it is the first one with an actual date."

"Do you think they will go through with it?"

"Who knows," Anna responded after a pause. Her eyes were hollowed, darkened around the edges like someone who had not had a proper night's sleep and she held the untouched bottle of beer in her hand uncomfortably and as far from her body as she could, like someone who wasn't a drinker but accepted the drink out of politeness.

Then with a burst of short, empty laughter she said to me, "Operation Murambatsvina."

I looked at her blankly.

She smiled and said, "Operation clear out the rubbish!"

Anna put the bottle down next to the wall and mumbled something about needing sleep. I wondered how she would be able to get any rest with the noise of the party blaring.

The festivities and the food lasted until the early hours of the morning. The next day, bleary-eyed, I unpacked my things and stashed the box and money back in their home beneath the floorboards. As I emptied my bags, I felt the tension in my shoulders begin to relax.

I lay in bed that night and thought about the people from the box. I was trying to piece together another puzzle from the box: the book. I had read it and re-read it and really could not understand its significance. It was a book about mythical dwarf-like creatures that set out to reclaim their ancestral land – not the romance I had been hoping for. Perhaps I was searching for symbolism and meaning where there simply was none.

I heard the screeching first. Shrieks were coming from the Congolese bedroom and I heard doors banging and people crying out in confusion. I sat up, my heart thumping. Cecile and Marie-Eve were wailing and I heard rough male voices growling in a language I did not understand. Redefine had arrived, a day late.

The first thing I did was flip up my mattress. I needed to get my money and Sarah's box. I didn't care if I left without my clothes, but I needed my money. I needed Sarah and Mandla. I had just taken my pen knife out of my jeans when I heard the fabric of my scarf door tear apart.

He was a burly man dressed in black military clothes and waving a baton in his hand. He banged it against my wall and a clump of black mouldy ceiling dropped to the ground at his feet. We both stared at it in surprise.

"Get out. Take what you can in your hands."

"I need to fetch something first," I pleaded, trying to get to the floor board.

"Are you stupid?" he spat at me, "Take your clothes and get out."

"I have to –"

He cut me off by smashing the baton against my face. I fell to the floor in shock and felt something watery slipping off my face and slopping on the floor. It was bright red. The smell of blood brought me back to Turbi but this time I was not an unarmed twelve-year-old. I got up and waved my pen knife.

"I first need to get something then I will leave."

He blasted the baton against my elbow sending agony shooting up my arm and the knife flying to the floor. He shoved me into the corridor and held the baton across my throat. With unbridled menace, he said, "And I told you to get out."

I gasped for breath beyond the choke-hold of the baton, and relived the moments before we left Turbi. My vision blurred. He was no longer wearing a uniform, he was no longer holding a baton – instead he was waving a panga and threatening to kill me and my aunt. My aunt was crouched on the floor begging for my life. She pleaded for him to take hers but to leave me unharmed. We had already lost Mwende – slaughtered at school with the rest of her friends earlier that day.

Like the men who killed off my village, for some reason this man decided against killing me, and released the baton. I clutched my throat, trying to breathe and saw an ashen Cecile cowering against the wall, gripping a soft toy in her hands, watching me.

The sheets had been ripped apart in the lounge and the mattress was being thrown out the window. Maria held Marie-Eve in her arms while Joseph's bloodied face was grim with determination as he moved to pick up Cecile. I was pushed out of the building by a less aggressive man, but I could feel his bullet proof vest rasp against my back.

The residents of Boston Heights sat outside the building that was now barricaded with wooden planks and barbed wire, all looking slightly dazed. Canvas bags, mattresses and clothes surrounded us as we crowded the pavement with nowhere to go. I sat on the edge of the pavement, alone, with nothing in my hands. Marie-Eve ran up to me and gave me some bright orange cheese puffs that she held in her hand, sensing that I had nothing to eat.

My money and the tin box were left in 44 Boston Heights and there was no way I would be able to reach them. I had lost everything. Already I had to force myself to shove Mandla and Sarah back into the box and bury them. I could not grieve over what I had lost; I had to find a way to survive.

The worst was seeing the sparkling cars purposefully slow down to watch us, the spectacle, with strange looks of satisfaction on their faces. They gazed at us and our meagre belongings. They did not see the life and laughter of the night before. They did not see the love and joy of Cecile and Marie-Eve. They did not see what treasures we left behind us, buried in Boston Heights. Instead they saw rubbish being cleared out. We were alone.

Catherine Jarvis was born in Johannesburg, but spent the first ten years of her life in the bustling metropolis of Mafikeng. She went on to study English Literature at Wits University, and then spent a couple of years abroad, before becoming an English teacher at a high school in Johannesburg. When Catherine is not teaching or marking, which is rather a rare occasion, she enjoys the company of books, her three cats, her family and her husband. The time she finds to write is precious indeed, and so she feels profoundly honoured to have been included in this anthology.

A Serving of Honey

Bryen Walter Kangwagye

There was pain in her eyes; her bruised lip hurt. Her thigh remained slightly painful, but her leg held firm her stride. Theresa watched her daughter rush off with a plastic bag and a knife to the task she had summoned her to do. Unlike cooking and cleaning, harvesting honey was an errand Clara accomplished with some success. It required agile hands and springy feet to get to the roof-hanging beehive, both of which Theresa lacked on account of her injuries. In the absence of sugar, she needed a sweetener for tea, and with Masaka Province under siege from the RPF rebels there would be no shopping for that delicacy from the abandoned towns.

Theresa's earliest memory concerned all her grandma had to say about honey. While she sat by her side one windy day when she was little, the old woman had placed three gourds before her tiny feet, the first filled with blood from a bull, the second with salted water, the third empty. She gave her the first gourd to drink from. With the second she washed Theresa's face and arms. She then placed the third gourd in Theresa's little hands.

"Grandma, it is empty," she said.

"I know," the old woman replied, "Go! Fill it with honey. Find him who will breathe your breath and spit on your tongue. He is the one to whom you will serve your honey. And may the winds from the east bring him to you, he who will eat from your calabash. Go child, go through the world. And all your life the winds will guide you."

The superstitious woman had sadly died soon after, leaving Theresa, her sister and her mother alone to farm the land of their inheritance. But the sisters could not shrug off the lure of the city, until they finally traded green landscapes for the torture of concrete and smog.

She stared disagreeably at the dirty cooking pans and dishes in the kitchen enclosure outside the main house, before washing them and setting them on a shelf to dry. She looked over to the front yard, and was glad to see Abbé engaging his two comrades-in-arms in animated discussion. They stood outside the old outhouse across the yard. Within its rafters was the beehive where Clara was harvesting the honey. Theresa felt safe for the first time in many days, smiling as she returned to her task of cooking.

She set a water-filled saucepan on the tree stump that served as a chair, before covering its top with a banana leaf. With the speed and masterly precision of one seasoned in the art of cooking, she filled the stove with black charcoal pellets from a half-empty sack and stacked a few fallen dry leaves gathered from the surrounding terrain into the small kiln. Next she lit a match and coaxed it in with the leaves. They soon picked up the flames and sent smoke billowing over the kitchen shade. She squinted her eyes through the smoke as she continued to feed the fire with twisted pieces of paper from an old *Rwanda New Times* newspaper. With the smoke trickling down as the charcoal burned red, she set the saucepan full of water onto the stove and sat down on the tree stump, waiting for it to boil. Presently her thoughts returned to the object of her joy.

She had first met Abbé thirteen years ago. Within a short time his affections for her had grown to such an extent that he was able to plead that she give up her job as a prostitute. It was clear that he enjoyed her company and was intrigued by her charm, but for Theresa he was the most powerful force in her young and restless world.

Their bond culminated in her pregnancy, which worsened complications that Theresa had begun to suspect. By way of rumours, she had heard that Abbé did some reconnaissance work for a rebel outfit opposed to the Rwandan government. When he confessed to his involvement, Theresa chose to accept it as a mild interruption; a wound that would heal no matter the hurt it caused. This was new joy. This was new pain. Both feelings were at their most jagged in her head. They always tried to make the most of the little time they had. Owing to the lengths of separation they both endured, it was easy to avoid tiffs and to enjoy one another's company in the first few days of their reunion. Tonight was one such night, when anxious mental agitation was replaced with calm sobriety, anger with adoration, dislike with fondness, and quarrels with kisses. The last time she had seen him, he had offered a hurried explanation, something about urgent rebel matters that needed immediate attention. Despite his absence, he promised to contribute substantially to her purse. But the money did not come and her savings dwindled.

Clara came bounding into the kitchen enclosure with a small plastic bag filled with honey. Her face and limbs covered in a thin film of soot.

"I hope the honey was not dirtied by the smoke? You might have to go back for more," Theresa warned.

Clara scanned the contents of the plastic bag with widening eyes. The unhappy prospect of having to return prompted her to set the sweet harvest carefully on the counter, just in case any further handling destroyed it. The removal of honey from the hive required lighting a dull fire in the outhouse with dried grass so that the smoke rose to the hive in the rafters, dazing the bees till the honey could be scooped harmlessly from the combs. Clara's upper arms were marked by several stings. She scratched at them as she peered into the saucepan. Seeing nothing edible, she retrieved a banana from a cluster beside a pail of water and quickly ate it.

Tired, she yawned. The exertion caused her to lean against a wooden post, one of four poles that supported the kitchen enclosure.

Theresa watched her with incredulous eye as she unwrapped a paper bag containing cassava flour.

"Your face is as black as nightfall. Go get cleaned," she said.

Clara showed her the few bee stings that were the trophies of her efforts and proclaimed how high she had climbed, before running off into the house.

When the water boiled, Theresa poured some flour into it and carefully stirred it with a pestle until the flour gelled to a thick white paste. She scooped the posho into a bowl which she placed onto a small rickety table. Next she placed freshly cut beef chunks into a pan, and a minute later added freshly cut vegetables, before returning to her seat while stirring the pan's contents. Salt would be added a little later when the beef started sizzling. It took a while before she could recall where she had placed it.

Looking for the salt reminded her again of Abbé all those years ago, of searching for him when he did not return. She had not been able to find him. After all hope of seeing Abbé again was gone, she finally moved in with Kichacha, her older sister, and her eight year old son, Kengi. They shared the same narrow nose and brown eyes, but that was all that they held in common. Kichacha was of fair build and more aggressive than Theresa, but only with regard to the things that her hands found to do. She maintained a general pessimism, yet her facial features were warm and flexible despite the stiff lines on her sun-kissed forehead. Her tresses were worn thicker than Theresa's, but shorter, so that there was little need to tie them back. Kichacha was slightly taller, bustier, and much broader at the hips. Despite her size, there was more speed and rest-lessness in her every action. Perhaps owing to her failed marriage, Kichacha observed her world through shattered glass, referring often with cynicism to life's rarely positive momentum. Listening to her, one thought she held up half the sky on her back. Her many burdens required lifting. She was alarmed when it rained, as this meant tireless mopping of her shack's flooded floor; she hated taxi fares – their rates were always unfairly high; she loathed men – they rarely played a part in their children's lives. It was to this end that she addressed Theresa one sunny day as they sat on the only bed in her single-roomed dwelling.

'Now I told you never to trust men,' she rebuked her younger sister. "I told you not to date your customers, but you did anyway. *But he loves me*, so you said!" She rounded it off with a pinch of scorn. "Hah! Now he is gone, the coward, all because you became pregnant!" She spat on the floor.

Although Theresa's earlier occupation had placed much risk on her health, it nevertheless could be trusted to pay the bills more consistently than the meagre resources that slum dwellers' occupations provided.

By now, thoughts of Abbé had graduated from tender to coarse. He had made promises about a life together, but had instead abandoned her. She believed now that though he had sworn his devotion to her, he had, in fact, forsaken her. And since he was not around to defend himself, she was able to believe the worst of him. She finally saw his opinions to be more like water at the bottom of a canoe, always moving from side to side, never still. Her motive for keeping a photo of him had been called into question, but for reasons she could not express, she kept it. It was only with much difficulty that one rainy day she ventured to the Old Taxi Park with the intention to investigate the whereabouts of any Rwandan tradesman that might have been known to frequent the area.

But her enquiries brought no information other than the fact that the man in her photo had not been seen in the city for many weeks. *Perhaps he was not at fault and was only held up by the rebellion*, she thought. Worse, perhaps he was dead, some traders she had spoken to had guessed. She kept the photo, reasoning her child would love a photo of her father. The matter was settled then. For seven years she stayed with her sister and maintained a textile shop in the less wealthy section of Kampala, by the end of which period they were able to afford to relocate to more affluent housing.

Steam billowed from the pan as she poured some water onto the beef. She placed a lid over it and set about chopping leafy green vegetables into a smaller pan. Unlike in Rwanda where she had bought all her vegetables from the market in peace time, in Uganda much of their food was harvested from their mother's farm.

They had abandoned their new city quarters to take possession of the farm after their mother had died from a long illness. In the next five years they invested all their resources into the success of the cattle and the crops, realising almost immediately the bounty of their new farm's financial reward.

Nyakatare, their wealthy uncle, upon seeing the vast productivity of their inheritance, made a substantial offer for their farm, but the sisters could not be convinced to part with it. He was so persuasive, however, that over the course of a few months the women were soon convinced to enter into negotiations after he presented a skilfully crafted written agreement that was mostly to their satisfaction. One key ingredient in winning them over to his enterprise was the promise to facilitate their transportation to Rwanda, the land of their ancestors and only surviving relatives, a trip they had long planned, but for lack of proper financing had forever postponed. He promised to secure their settlement in the town of their mother's birth. Theresa looked forward to staying close to their only surviving aunt, Béata, who had taken care of their mother throughout her illness. Now much older herself, Béata required the attentions of a constant nurse.

The sisters proved to be consummate businesswomen. They led their uncle through an hour of strenuous negotiations and methodical calculations on the value of the farm and its instalments. They declared he was buying a piece of heaven, he remained convinced it was a nondescript spot on earth. Kichacha quoted bold sums to counter his inadequate price ranges, all the while over-emphasizing the value of their crops and herd. Agreement was finally reached. The two women became proud owners of a huge bundle of cash.

Theresa placed the green vegetables onto the stove after the meat was cooked. She added a sprinkling of oil, salt, and water. She churned the leaves for a few minutes until they were tender, before placing them onto a plate with the aid of a slotted spoon.

She examined her work with arms akimbo: spiced beef sauce to be balanced with subtle posho and greens; a jar of drinking water to wash it all down; a cup of tea for whoever desired; a calabash filled with honey freshly harvested for sweetener. This was the closest to a feast she could put together in a time of war.

Clara came out again, done with her washing. She stood staring at Theresa with odd satisfaction, running her hands across her face and upper arms to drain little droplets of water. The fringes of her face, hair and dress were still covered in soot. A touch upon her dirty skirts to wipe her wet hands only blackened them anew.

"Owaye! Go back and bathe. Take that dirty dress off. Take a full shower," Theresa said firmly, as a pouting Clara rushed back into the house.

Theresa's only regret of relocating here was bringing her daughter along with her at the worst of times. The Interahamwe subjected their victims to the most brutal hackings. Theresa had found difficulty in shielding Clara from seeing the brutally hacked dead bodies in the streets and grass fields. The dead were everywhere; the dead were all around the living.

Upon arrival in Rwanda's Masaka Province their legacy of cash put it in the sisters' power to maintain board in a small inn for a few days. They soon purchased the vacant plot that neighboured their aunt's farm. Its garden was full of weeds; its large kraal housed no animals. The sisters promptly populated it with a small herd of one old bull and six cows.

In the breeding season the old bull inseminated all the cows. While some did not take kindly to his approach, a few got pregnant. The others returned to the bull for a second chance at love, but were promptly turned away by the angry beast whose temperament had become too unpredictable. He was soon sold for beef and replaced with a much younger beast who, suffice to say, exceeded expectations.

A couple with a large herd resided in the other neighbouring farm. It was aunt Béata who suggested the sisters hire the services of that couple's eldest son, Kantano, to tend their cattle.

He brought to the job his vast semi-nomadic experience and commenced with great enthusiasm. He easily developed a bond with Kengi who accompanied him on his herding trips to other pastures. In the course of Kantano's daily labours they moved from place to place, taking the cattle to lands not claimed as any single person's property, uninhabited grasslands, returning home only at sundown.

As the herd slowly grew, the ladies got busy selling dairy milk at the local market, together with the maize and green bananas they harvested from the farm.

Clara had an insatiable love for dance and acting. Her voracious appetite for all things dramatic led to many selections for lead roles in plays at school. On sports day she took to running the competitive races, registering only mild success. Yet she attempted everything worth attempting, for the troubling coughs and ill health that tortured her early years had long vanished, leaving behind a vigorous pair of lungs.

The rains came two months late, their absence in the village visible in the brown countryside. As a famine took hold, the cows had to be herded many miles further from the village to graze. The two village wells had dropped significantly in levels so that man and beast saw each other as competition for every drop that descended from the heavens or issued from the earth.

Though superstition was not as prevalent as it had been in their former Ugandan hometown, rumours, fuelled by the village witchdoctor, went round that the gods were not pleased with the new road the government had constructed through their village.

The government's men with their elephant machines had come unannounced and displaced those people that lived by the planned road's route. They dug out a huge pathway in the valley, and covered it with stones and a black paste. That was the only sprinkle of modernism in the entire village and surrounding hills. To passing travellers the area seemed a tranquil oasis of uninterrupted nature, until the few huts sighted about announced human habitation.

If the local witchdoctor had his way, that road would have been destroyed, for he believed that the gods were not pleased with the noise that traffic brought into their once quiet village. This, he maintained, was the reason the rains did not come. He proclaimed the only thing that would end hostilities with the gods would be a sacrifice consisting of a portion of every household's harvests.

Those that believed him, which numbered a fair minority, wholeheartedly gave their portion. The sisters, along with many other families, were opposed to the scheme. Soon there was a growing disenchantment from the witchdoctor's few supporters. The trouble with this minority was that they were the most vocal, counting the Prefect of Masaka, the local superintendent of police, and the mayor of the town among their numbers.

Occasionally when Grégoire, the witchdoctor, chanced upon the sisters in the street or market, he treated them in an unceremonious and contemptuous manner. And although Theresa thought the magic quack was an insufferable bore who was eternally self-obsessed, his endless heckling nevertheless unsettled their lives. Yet they were determined to stand on principle. Appeals from a few friends could not persuade them otherwise.

Grégoire became their arch enemy. He always sought ways to discredit them, until finally he got his chance when the President's plane was shot down. Immediately after his assassination, the country was engulfed in a war.

The frenzied killings of Tutsis and Hutus bore no sign of ceasing. The RPF rebels mounted a spirited campaign to crush the government forces. The sisters were caught in a war. Kichacha and Kengi's return from Kigali, where they had gone to find a market for the vast quantities of plantain their farm produced, was halted. Theresa wished her relations were safe, but she would have no way of telling until the war ended. Grégoire and his machete-wielding militiamen came to her farm and held the property under siege before Theresa could escape. They searched the property, including the outhouse into which Clara had disappeared, but did not find the girl.

The terror in Theresa's eyes requires no telling as Grégoire dragged her onto her bed. She tried to scream, though she knew it would amount to nothing, but Grégoire's hand held her lips tightly shut. She searched for wriggle room, but his weight above her was too great. The thought of a life after this rape was incomprehensible to her. In despair, she shut her eyes tight as he lifted her dress up and tore her underwear. Then, for what seemed like an eternity, he rummaged through his pants. Nothing happened.

Despite the awfulness of her situation, Theresa could not help but be surprised by the inactivity. More shuffling and grunts of frustration met her ears, which intensified when he got off her chest and straddled her. When she finally opened her eyes, she discovered that he had failed to summon himself to the task. He exerted all effort to elicit a response from his leaky pipe, but it could not be easily persuaded. Theresa was glad for his misfortune.

He tied her hands to the bed post and exited the house, returning half an hour later with a skin sack that he threw onto the floor. The impact threw its lid open, spilling numerous cowry shells, rocks, nuts and bolts, plus a few blunt knives onto the floor; the tools of his dark trade.

The witchdoctor quickly laid them out in an order only understood by him, and commenced an odd chant in a language Theresa could not comprehend.

She figured he hoped to channel some energy from the shells to his pants. She started her own silent prayer, imploring God to help her.

Then Grégoire opened his reddened eyes suddenly, staring blankly at the closed window as if struck by an idea. He smiled slyly at her and vacated the room again with a knife in hand.

Silence befell the house again. Theresa tried with all her effort to wrench her hands free. She sat up on the bed and stretched one foot across the floor to grab a rusted knife. Just then he returned, causing her to drop back onto the bed.

Grégoire threw a terrified chicken onto the floor. The creature had its legs restrained with rope, and got no relief from frantically flapping its wings.

"Blood of chicken can replace blood of goat. A sprinkling of it into your mouth and I will be cured of your curse," he said as he paced about the creature, his eyes glaring into hers.

He beheaded the chicken and cut a gaping hole through its torso before extracting its internal organs. Then he thrust a blood-soaked hand at her face, smearing it with the creature's warm blood.

Despite taking all his clothes off, and after many loud entreaties to his god in numerous chants that reverberated throughout the walls of the room, his leaky pipe still hung loose.

He grew ever more desperate. He shredded her dress. He stared at her nakedness in the hope of getting aroused. There was still nothing. Grégoire was in crisis. He burst into such a flood of tears. The thought that he might have made an unrealistic assessment of his own abilities crippled him. He flew into a murderous rage, and administered a ferocious combination of punches. His kicks struck Theresa's torso hard. She passed out. He raised his machete up to strike her head. Gunshots rang out from the valley below. For a moment he froze to listen. The loud wailings of his militia running from an assault disoriented his thoughts for a brief moment. He dropped the blade. More gunshots. He grabbed his clothes and began to dress. A bullet grazed through the slit in the window and burrowed into his forehead. Grégoire staggered back out of the room before landing in a heap in the front yard.

Many hours later Theresa woke to a silent house and saw Abbé hovering over her. After more than a decade of searching he had finally found her. Kigali had fallen, and the rebels now pursued the retreating machete-wielding gangs throughout the countryside.

Abbé sat watching her closely, unable to find the right words. Soon he told her how he had searched for her at her old town house; how he had searched for her at Kichacha's slum house; how he had missed her by a few hours when he searched for her at their Ugandan farm. Theresa looked away, covering her face in her bruised hands. When he finally made an attempt to embrace her, she recoiled towards the wall.

Clara emerged from the roof of the old outhouse that had been her hiding place. Her skill at scaling the ceiling had saved her from the wrath of Grégoire's blade. She lay beside her mother throughout the night.

For the next two days Abbé and two of his comrades-in-arms stayed guard at her home, the bulk of his battalion having been sent ahead to pursue the militia. They fed on only yellow bananas and maize from her plantation, reserving the hot stove for the quick tasks of tea-making and boiling drinking water. The three men spent much of their time repulsing attacks from militiamen with their AK47s and Uzi Carbines.

By the second day of her recuperation, Theresa could walk, albeit with a limp, around the farmhouse. She introduced her daughter to her father. He regarded her with warm affection, and the two chatted throughout the day. It was while she stood gazing at the distant horizon by the mango tree that he walked up to her and kissed her bruised lip. She winced and pushed him away.

"I thought I was dead. How did you bring me back?" she asked.

"I breathed air into your lungs," he said.

By the afternoon of the third day, Theresa abandoned her bed with a renewed strength to exert herself in the kitchen. She intended to prepare a more exciting meal than the fruit they had become accustomed to. Fried food would suit the man that had breathed her breath and spat on her tongue.

With all the food finally prepared, she placed the small dishes onto a table by the mango tree. At the sight of food the three men paused in mid-conversation, glad for their first cooked meal in many days. She set three plates beside the dishes alongside two jars of hot tea and water, three plastic cups, and a gourd of honey for sweetener carefully skimmed from the plastic bag.

"Come. Eat," she said. They all converged at the small table, setting their guns on the grass to free their hands.

Clara munched on a few bits before disappearing back into the house. In a few minutes the food was eaten, and the men took turns thanking her profusely. While Abbé's friends helped themselves to water, he settled for a hot cup of tea. As Theresa watched him, he placed a spoonful of honey into his drink, stirred and drank it all up.

Theresa drew closer to him. His hands held her waist, not as lightly as water at the bottom of a canoe, but likewise swayed her exultantly from side to side. Their lips merged in a kiss. And there was no pain in her eyes. Her bruised lip did not hurt.

Bryen Walter Kangwagye lives in Kampala, Uganda and works as an IT Officer at Uganda's Central Bank. He holds a BSc in Mechanical Engineering from Makerere University and an MSc in Information Technology from the University of East London. He spends his free time reading novels, screenplays, and writing stories.

Black Coffee without Sugar

Lauri Kubuitsile

Leon looks down along the steam table and is not surprised by what he sees. A meeting for head teachers in the Central District and he could have guessed what was in each stainless steel pan before they lifted the lids. Bogobe, Tastic rice (overcooked), paletshe, too-dry seswaa, fried-to-death chicken ("one piece only, please") and flabby iceberg lettuce swimming in a sea of vinaigrette. What can he say really? Free food is one of the perks of the job. You shouldn't look a gift horse in the mouth, whatever that might mean. He smiles as the big woman behind the steam table drops a chicken wing on his ceramic white plate with a sound much like metal hitting metal. He reminds himself to not even try his teeth on that one, he suspects his new bridge won't stand up to it.

He turns to the tables scattered around the hotel dining room. He spots an empty one by the window and heads for it. He knows it's not good for business to be unsociable, it is word of mouth that gets him these gigs, but he hopes whoever sits with him will be more interested in eating than talking. His day started badly and he needs some quiet time to think through a few things.

He woke up that morning to his wife, Mara, sitting at the dining room table in the dark drinking black coffee. Cold, black coffee. From the day before even. No milk or sugar like normal people. Just black and oily. She knew he had a conference two hours away, why did she have to drink cold, black coffee in the dark on a conference day? He didn't like to admit it, but he was angry when he saw her sitting there. He thought she was being a bit selfish.

He considered sneaking back to their bedroom and getting ready without his morning tea, but realised that wasn't a reasonable plan since he'd eventually have to leave the house through the front door, which would mean passing through the dark dining room in any case. It was one thing if you didn't see your wife drinking cold, black, day-old coffee in the dark, another thing all together if you saw her and ignored it, and a step too far if she knew that you had seen her.

So he stepped carefully into the dining room, still in his bathrobe, and said, "Are you okay, Mara?"

"Sure, yes. I'm fine."

She did not turn in his direction when she said it though. She just sat holding the cup in both her hands as if it was warming them, and staring at the wall of the dining room, at the painting of a lion he'd been given as a gift at one of his seminars. It was a nice enough painting, a bit too safari lodge-ish for his taste, but not a painting a person needed to study to get the meaning. It was a male lion lying down, his paws in front, his mane flowing around his face. The look on his face had a hint of disdain. Leon guessed someone might spend a bit of time thinking about that, about what he was so disdainful about, but not a long time. There were only so many things a lion might be disdainful about and once the list was exhausted there really wasn't much else the painting had to offer the viewer. But yet Mara stared at it and it looked like she'd been staring at it for a good long time.

The cold, black, day-old coffee and the staring at a painting that really did not warrant staring at was more than enough for Leon to accept that his wife really wasn't fine. But he knew that anyway. He'd been ignoring the idea for some time, thinking it would all pass, but then she ran away last month, ran further than usual. Over the border to Lephalale where he found her staying at a lodge they sometimes stayed at together. Initially, when the police told him she had crossed the border, he thought maybe she'd run away with someone, maybe that manager at the Spar she liked talking to all the time. But he wasn't there. It was only her. Sitting on the made bed, her hands on her lap. When Leon arrived she said, "Hello, dear how was your day?" as if he was coming home from a seminar and not like she had run away for three days.

Leon asked her why she had run away but he never got a straight answer. She'd run away before, but to nearby places. Crossing the border was making everything serious, and she'd been gone for three days, that was a long time. He had been very worried, even thought that she might be dead. He had to get the police involved, something he didn't like doing. It made it all too official for him.

They came home and things went mostly back to normal until this morning. He called the odd things Mara did 'spells' and he'd been happy she'd been free of her spells for some time. Not that she was her normal old Mara-self between her spells, but she did things that didn't cause too much trouble. She didn't sit in the dark and look at lions or slip away over the border. She was just quiet and distracted. They could both live with that.

He promised himself he'd sort it all out when he got home, he didn't have time to deal with it in the morning or he'd be late for his seminar. Instead he'd opened the dining room drapes, gave Mara new hot coffee with milk and sugar the way she liked it when she was herself and buttered toast with the crusts cut off. He kissed her and said, "I'll see you this evening."

"Yes, dear," she said, still studying the disdainful lion, her head slightly askew as if she was attempting to listen to a faint voice she was struggling to locate.

His thoughts are interrupted by the very man, of all of the people in the workshop, Leon hoped would not come to talk to him. He spotted him first thing in the morning. Every workshop has one of these types. Leon calls them the know-it-all, attention seekers. He really doesn't need this guy today.

He is a thin, tiny man with a nervous mouth. He looks about mid-fifties, Leon guesses. His suit jacket is shiny with wear, his pinkie fingernail long and dirty. His eyes bloodshot, but not from alcohol, Leon knows these types, too self righteous for alcohol. He holds out his hand to Leon. "Franklin. Franklin Moetse."

"Nice to meet you," Leon says.

"Rre Modise, that was a fantastic talk you gave us just now, I doubt I could have done better myself," Franklin says too loudly, looking around to see who is listening to him, as he sits down in the chair next to Leon's even though the chair opposite is vacant. Leon's hopes fall even further because he can tell this man, this Franklin, is a toucher. Leon doesn't like being touched. Especially by strangers.

"Thank you," Leon says, smiling politely but hoping to keep the conversation limited. He looks around for anyone who might sit with them to dilute Franklin a bit. The queue at the steam table is finished and everyone seems to have found a seat elsewhere. Leon becomes busy with his food.

"I love a good motivational talk and you are fantastic. That thing you said about eagles flying and the tree in the forest, spot on, spot on, my brother." He slaps Leon on the back and lets his hand stay a few moments longer than it needs to.

Leon eats his food even though the rice has obviously been burnt at some point and the seswaa has no salt. He looks around for salt on the tables, but there is none.

"I'd love to have you to my school. My teachers are all a bunch of whiners and lazy sorts. This is why the school gets such poor results. I'd fire the lot but you know these government workers. You've got a talent to inspire. You could have been a minister. God knows our minister down at our church... I go to the UCCSA, you know, not any of those funny churches with Nigerian ministers and such. That's not a church, is it now Leon? UCCSA, now there's a proper kind of church, not one all full of foreigners and such. Don't you think so?"

He holds his hand on Leon's shoulder and looks him in the eye expecting an answer. "Well..." Leon tries. "I don't know much about churches to be honest."

"What was I saying now... oh yes, well I can tell you one thing, our Pastor Kgalemang could take a few pages from your book on motivation. He makes a person not want to even step into the church with his sermons. Boring. Dead boring. I've tried to give him some tips but he can't be bothered. He knows what he's doing he says, but I doubt it. It's all about motivation and you really do have a gift. A bit like me really."

Franklin tears at his chicken as if it has offended him in some way. Leon wonders what Mara is doing at home. He hopes she hasn't wandered off somewhere. She used to work; she had her own hair salon. It was quite well known and was doing very well. Then one day about two years ago, she woke up and she didn't go to the salon. She didn't give a reason, but she never went there again. Leon hired a manager for the shop and he checked it every once in a while. He wanted to keep it ready in case Mara decided to go back to work one day. If the reason that made her stop disappeared.

He didn't know what to think of it all. Mara had been such a happy young woman. She grew up in Shoshong with her parents and three sisters, Mara being the youngest. She and Leon met at university. It wasn't a lightning bolt kind of love, just a slow, steady rain kind of love. They'd had a happy life together until she changed, until the spells started.

Those early days, he'd worked for government but got caught up with the wrong people and had to leave. He regretted all that. It was hard on both of them. He had to rebuild himself, but Mara managed. She was always positive and supportive. After it all blew over, she was the one who gave him the idea to try motivational speaking. He'd listened to all of the tapes from folks like Miles Monroe, Jack Canfield, and the like and learned quite a bit. In Botswana it was easy to convince people you were something if you said it confidently enough and Leon was almost always confident so he did pretty well. He had good speaking skills.

He could admit now that at first he wasn't sincere about any of it. He didn't really believe people could just wish things to be a certain way and then they magically were. He still felt pretty much the same way except that he knew now that his talks helped some people. Some people came into the room one way and came out a different way, a better way. Once he realised his talks did that he took them a bit more seriously.

Soon he was the pre-eminent motivational speaker in the country, mostly because there were no others. He got invited to posh workshops held by organisations like DeBeers and to government seminars, workshops on team building and productivity. He was always busy and making a very good income. People forgot all about his messing up when he worked for government. Batswana tended to have short, forgiving memories and Leon was thankful for that.

Franklin is, not surprisingly, still talking though Leon, thankfully, misses most of it. "… and you know it really is all about how we look at things, isn't it, Leon my brother?" Franklin's greasy chicken hands don't stop him from patting Leon's arm. "You must just put the right spin on things. Like that calling problems challenges. You see there? That's very clever, my brother, that's very clever. Now it's just a question that must be answered instead of a wall you can't climb. It's good that. I wrote that down in my hardcover. I'm going to definitely use that when I get back to my school."

Leon wishes Franklin would notice that he isn't in the mood for talking, but these types never do. They only live in their tight prescribed worlds and to try and think how another person is feeling is as impossible for them as walking on the sun.

"Good. I'm glad you got something useful out of my talk," Leon says, moving his arm slightly so Franklin's hand slips to the tablecloth.

"Oh yes, oh yes." Franklin stands up. Is he going? Leon hopes. "I'm getting sweets. Should I bring for you?" Franklin asks. Leon's hopes dashed, he nods wearily and Franklin disappears.

Leon looks out the window, watching the cars passing on the busy road in front of the hotel. All sorts of cars, on the main highway, the A1, people rushing north and south. Busy with their lives. All sorts of people. He starts thinking about his wife back home. He should have skipped this workshop. He should have stayed with her. He knew Mara was not okay and hadn't been for some time, but he never spoke it out loud. Neither one of them spoke about how their lives had changed, neither admitted something was wrong. He'd ask her questions. Was she okay? Why didn't she go to the salon? Why did she keep running away? What was wrong with him that made her want to go?

Lephalale was the farthest she'd gone. He'd once found her sitting by the pool at Gaborone Sun, dangling her feet in the water after disappearing for most of the day. He'd been frantically looking for her and called a friend who told him that he had seen her there. Another time she was at the nearby primary school, swinging on one of the swings. The headmistress had called him, they knew each other from walking their dogs. She often passed him on the road in front of the school. She had a very fat Jack Russell; they had an old toothless Maltese poodle. Nonofo, the headmistress, called him on his cell that day.

"Your wife's been swinging on our swings since first period. The kids are going out for lunch. There are only four swings and they're in high demand," she said.

"Okay. I'm coming," Leon said.

He'd found Mara swinging high, high as the swing would take her, her legs pumping, her bare feet covered in red dust. Her eyes cast to the clear blue sky.

"Hi," he'd said.

"Hi Leon."

When she saw him she stopped pumping her legs and let them hang. Leon watched as the swing slowed and eventually came to a stop.

"Do you want to go home now?" he asked her.

"Sure," she said.

He watched her pick up her shoes, one flung off to one side, one to the other. She carried them as they walked to the car. His cellphone beeped. It was a message from Nonofo seeing if he wanted to go for a drink. He sms-ed back: "I'll call you." He never did. He found her behaviour very opportunistic, something he didn't like.

He wished he knew what the problem was with Mara and how he could get it to stop. He just never knew what to expect and he didn't like that kind of uncertainty. He tried to be patient but sometimes he wanted to shake her and tell her to stop it. To just be normal again. When she disappeared over the border, there were a few hours as he waited in their big house that he was sure she was dead. In those hours he felt strange. He guessed he felt sad a bit. But he was surprised that he didn't feel overwhelming grief at the prospect of losing his wife of seventeen years. He sat in that quiet house, sure she was dead, and what he felt most of all was relief. Relief that it was finally over. The mystery not solved, but at least it was all over. And then the police called and it wasn't.

Franklin comes back with the sweets. Leon is happy to see it's canned sliced peaches and tinned cream. He doesn't want to think about what the catering staff would have done to custard. "Here you go, Leon my brother," Franklin says setting the dishes on the table. "Do you have kids there, Leon?"

"No... no I don't. We never had kids, my wife and I." He tries to let the rudeness of Franklin's question flow over him and away.

"That's too bad. You know that bit on goal-setting techniques I'm going to use on my son. Now there's one lazy boy, if I do say so myself. He's in need of some motivation and goal setting. Does nothing at all that boy, no good if you ask me. But a father has to keep trying."

Leon watches as Franklin brings the spoon to his mouth with a peach slice covered in cream. He slurps all of the cream off and then eats the bare, orange peach slice left on the spoon. Each time. Over and over. An awful slurpy sound. Leon doesn't want to watch, he finds the entire method unpalatable, but he can't turn away. It is such an uncivilised and rude way of eating. As if no one else matters.

This man acts as if he listened to Leon's talk, as if he learned something. But he hasn't. He is ungrateful and so selfish. He has a son but he speaks of him so disparagingly. Nothing is up to this man's standards. All their problems, not his. Can he see nothing? Is he so solidly opaque that not a sliver of light can enter?

Franklin scoops up another peach slice covered in cream and Leon's hand shoots out. He grabs a hold of Franklin's thin, bony wrist and the spoon heaped with canned peaches and cream stands still in mid-air. Franklin looks at Leon. First he smiles, thinking it is some sort of joke, a game, but then he sees the firm resolve on Leon's face.

"Hey, let go of my hand," Franklin says. He struggles to pull his hand free but Leon holds tightly. The peach and the cream spill onto the tablecloth, but still he holds tightly. He feels as if he might never let go, that he shouldn't. Franklin's face fills with fear. He looks around for help in the near-empty dining room.

One of the workshop organisers comes over to their table. A stern woman with a shelf of breasts says to Leon, "Anything wrong, Mr Modise?"

Leon looks up at her smiling, still holding the smaller man's hand. "No, everything is fine."

He looks back at Franklin who knows from Leon's eyes he should not speak. The organiser moves on, as well as the few straggling participants, now called for their afternoon session.

Leon throws Franklin's hand to the table with force, the glasses rattle.

Franklin stands up and backs away from Leon, rubbing his wrist. "You're crazy, do you know that?" he says in a small voice with no force behind it. He disappears out the door.

The empty dining room becomes quiet, only the knocking of dishes in some far off kitchen can be heard. Leon turns back to the window, calm again, his hands resting lightly on the table. He watches the cars rushing north and south. Rushing, rushing to their places, wherever they are, to whatever waits for them.

Lauri Kubuitsile is a full-time, award-winning writer living in Botswana. She has more than twenty published books (in South Africa, Botswana and overseas) and many short stories published around the world. Among her books are The Fatal Payout *and* Mmele and the Magic Bones *(both currently prescribed in Botswana schools),* Signed, Hopelessly in Love *(chosen by O Magazine (RSA) as one of the 40 Best Reads in December 2011) and her most recent short story collection,* In the Spirit of McPhineas Lata and Other Stories *(Hands-on Books 2012). She has won or been shortlisted for numerous prizes among them she was shortlisted for the 2011 Caine Prize, twice won the The Golden Baobab Prize, and won Botswana Government's Botswerere Prize for Creative Writing in 2007. She blogs at* Thoughts from Botswana *(http://thoughtsfrombotswana.blogcpot.com)*

Where is the Tenderness?

Greg Lazarus

A few days before leaving, he went with his parents to get a dress suit. He'd never owned one before. Though he was shocked at the price, which was nearly what his dad earned in a week of repairing jewellery, his mother and father said they would pay for it happily. On the day of his departure, he hugged them tightly when they dropped him at the airport, and if he felt butterflies – could he cope with this, would he be regarded as a fool? – he tried to keep them down by repeating mantras to himself while on the plane, waiting for takeoff. *Stay strong*, he thought. *Be calm*. He missed his girlfriend desperately – his ex-girlfriend, he reminded himself. She had recently broken it off with him, saying that a long-distance relationship wouldn't work, and had immediately taken up with a teacher at Victoria Park High School – though she visited him just before he left, and gave him a book on meditating. He sat in the plane, the book on his lap. The author, a skeletal yogi, smiled gently up at him from the back cover.

The wonderful thing about his arrival at Cambridge was that, at least for a few days, he could stop thinking about his ex-girlfriend. Even though he sensed that her drumbeat could resume in his brain at any moment, for now she was silent as he went to the library or walked along the river Cam or picked up bits of Cambridge lore from his fellow new postgraduate students, a number of whom were socially awkward, like him. But they seemed comfortable with themselves, appeared to have settled into awkwardness early on, worked without ambivalence for scholarships, out-nerded everyone to get the marks it took to get here. At the University of Port Elizabeth he had not been quite sharp enough to put his thoughts together in new patterns, and had compensated for his lack of new ideas with many hours reading obscure books in the library, adding footnotes that grew longer than the essays themselves, until his philosophy teachers, exhausted at the sight of his persistent figure approaching them after a lecture, would give him firsts for essays to keep him away. Sometimes he would knock at their office doors, coming back later if they didn't answer, with his series of questions that were not questions but traps to get them to admit that he deserved a high mark, that he *must* do well.

In Cambridge he did his best to act the part. He acquired an accent that seemed to him crisp, clever and English. Perhaps as a result, he was often mistaken for a German or some other second-language speaker ("Your English is *very good*," a middle-aged woman who asked him for directions in the street told him, speaking slowly), but his voice was a work in progress.

A week after he arrived in Cambridge, once he had met his philosophy supervisor and discovered that he was expected to come up with research topics himself, a process that seemed to him somehow to miss the point – someone else sets the challenge, and then you meet it, and wait for another challenge to be handed down – there was a formal dinner for the new postgraduate students of his college. Smart in his dress suit, he found himself seated next to a garrulous Australian, already balding on the crown of his head, who seemed to have met everyone, to have explored every college and building, and to be jaded by it all, and ready to move on to the next thing. Opposite them was a girl called Kelly, whom at first he took, from the mental association with the outlaw Ned Kelly, to be a friend or girlfriend of the Australian, Todd. But then – after some questions in his new and still unstable accent – he discovered that she came from a suburb in London called Primrose Hill and that she had a delicate manner that could not easily be grasped, requiring that he continue looking at her and trying to work out what, behind her bobbed brown hair and green eyes, made her tick. Because certainly she seemed to be set on a different spring to other people – she was unimpressed by Cambridge, unlike all the other new graduate students, including him, who kept saying "Cambridge" and the name of their college as if they wanted to engrave it on their bones. He had even bought, from a grand shop on a corner with no other customers, a pair of cufflinks with his college's coat of arms on it, and then posted it to his parents. His scholarship did not really extend to the buying of silver cufflinks, but the thought of his father wearing the college cufflinks – his father had one shirt which took cufflinks, reserved for smart occasions – reassured him that all was going well.

This girl, though, said at the dinner that she might have made a mistake coming here, and that her boyfriend – here, as he listened, his mood modulated to a minor key, but still he maintained his air of thoughtful engagement

WHERE IS THE TENDERNESS?

– was having a much better time as a mountain guide in the Pyrenees. Up and down the Pyrenees the boyfriend went with his clients, and in his spare time he explored new crannies. Kelly explained all this quietly, holding a glass of red wine – the English, he had observed already, drank an astonishing amount of alcohol – in her slender hand while looking at him with her green, serene eyes. He explained to her in turn, eager to be interesting, some features of South Africa's new Constitution – somehow he worked this into the conversation – and she regarded his enthusiastic remarks without expression, except to nod occasionally. She was a law student, and he had expected her to find this interesting; it was unclear whether she was quiet because she knew it all already or for some other reason. He feared he might be boring her.

After dinner Todd, the restless Australian, proposed that they all go to his place for drinks – all of them, the new students at his portion of the table, including a tall American girl who frightened him because she had been at Harvard, an English guy, similarly intimidating, from Oxford, and a Hungarian student of mathematics whom he had seen on the street carrying a suitcase to and from his classes. They managed not to extend the invitation to the ancient, bellicose German professor of classics who was sitting at their section of the table. Her head was bowed under the weight of a long series of drinks, and she did not seem to be hearing very well at this time of the evening.

Out they went, into the main courtyard of the college, and he was hit by the icy English night air, which went through the jacket that he had purchased in Port Elizabeth as if it were made of tissue paper, and shocked him into chattiness. "You know," he said tipsily, his face frozen, "it's at a time like this, thousands of miles from home, that I really miss my ex-girlfriend."

"In a few months," said the Harvard girl, "you'll barely remember her name."

He could not reconcile her harsh confidence with the fact that she was his own age; the pieces did not fit together.

"Are you cold?" asked Kelly suddenly. She had come close to him as they walked across the midnight courtyard, past the ancient fountain at its centre, their breath steaming, drunk.

"Not at all," he said loudly, his teeth chattering in comic exaggeration. "What gave you that idea?"

"Hug your shoulders," she said. "And run." The two of them, embracing themselves, ran in ungainly fashion – he following her – in the direction of Todd's staircase, galloped up it and waited at the top, looking at each other in silent amusement until the rest arrived. He was panting but she was light, slender, and didn't seem to have felt this as exercise.

Todd's room proved to be messy, books scattered across the table, sweaters draped across the backs of the chairs, like he had lived there for years.

"Sherry?" he said opening a cupboard that contained a number of bottles of alcohol.

"Whisky," said the Oxford man. "We need the proper stuff at this time of night."

Todd accepted the rebuke, stored it away in his rapid acclimatisation mental unit, and drew from his cupboard a bottle of whisky. "I've been here the whole summer," he confided. "College let me come up early. Thought I'd get going with work, and obviously I needed plenty of drink for that." This seemed unfair and impressive, coming here a few months early, and as he looked at Todd he felt that he would often have this realisation, that there were others here who were in completely different leagues of commitment and cunning.

"Now that is delicious," said the Oxford man after a minute. "You like it?" he asked Kelly.

"I do." It was both affirmation and conclusion; Oxford opened his mouth, but there was nothing left to add.

He saw Kelly a few times on the street between lectures – he had still not identified any research topic, and was haunting the lecture theatres, hoping for an epiphany. Afflicted with the usual shyness, he did not approach her, and anyway his ex-girlfriend had burst back into his mind. He had been think-ing about her constantly, constructing imaginary conversations in which he persuaded her, by philosophical means, that she had been deeply mistaken to break it off with him. But late one afternoon, as he was walking back from his last lecture to his room in the college, Kelly approached him from an oblique angle and gravely asked, "What are you doing for dinner?" He jumped, and turned to see her impassive face. "I have pasta from Sainsbury's," she told him. "Keep me company?" They walked together to her flat, on the outskirts of town. She'd been put there, she explained as they went up the steps, because she'd registered for her degree at the last possible moment, when accommodation in the college was full. The college had found a place for her, she said, in this grotty old building.

He didn't find it grotty at all. The saggy sofa, dark brown cushions and soft brown carpeting that she called "so seventies" were a comfort to him, reminding him of childhood. The paper sphere dangling from the ceiling, glowing from the bulb within it, seemed exotic, mysterious.

She tossed a small amount of dry pasta, a handful of dense frilled pockets, into a steel pot of boiling water. Could that little bit really be for the two of them? But already she had turned away. "I've got some single-malt whisky."

"I don't drink whisky, thanks."

"You did at Todd's."

"I know, but I hate it." He felt, recklessly, as if it was essential to be completely honest with Kelly. She looked put out. "You go ahead," he said pleasantly. She poured herself a drink, but the mood had inflected a little.

"Your accent has changed since we last spoke," she said, a little unkindly. He sensed that it was his punishment for the whisky. She tilted her glass to take a sip.

"I know. I've been trying to sound clever."

Kelly snorted slightly into her whiskey, and then looked at him, amused. "Shall we have some music?"

"Sure." He had been to chapel choirs and organ recitals a few times a week since he'd arrived in Cambridge. He was awed by the music, but he found it remote, the rapture of others far away.

Kelly produced a portable CD player, put in a disc and then sat with the machine on the floor in front of her. "It's more comfortable than the sofa," she said. So he sat too, facing her, the CD player between them.

"My God," he said after a minute of yearning music, spilling as if from his very soul. "What is this?"

She looked surprised. "The Smiths."

"And they are?"

"Where have you been?"

There is a light, a lone voice sang again and again, that will never go out. Finally he closed his eyes. This brown and glowing flat, this girl who disconcerted him, this music, one of a million songs he had never heard – it was too much to manage at once. "I'll have whisky after all."

She nodded. "Laphroaig. Tastes like peat. You'll like it." And he did. That night they ate the pasta, which had taken an impossibly long time to boil. It was still hard, tightly curled, like the ears of some porcine race. Kelly passed on gossip: Harvard girl and Oxford guy had gotten together, but Oxford had suffered from a sudden runny tummy during a crucial moment, perhaps from a late night hamburger from the Van of Death that parked in the market from dusk to dawn, and the result was ruin and disaster. Kelly then spoke briefly about her boyfriend, who would visit Cambridge soon. She did not talk about her law degree, and listened to his confused thoughts about what he might try for his first philosophy research paper, now and then making a short and incisive remark. Then it was late, time to go home, and he stood up. "That was great, thanks."

"*Now* you're getting your South African accent back," she said.

"Oh." He tried not to sound disappointed.

"It's more you. Not that Prussian voice you had before. And anyway, I thought you were proud of being South African. Your Constitution and all." Her voice was teasing.

"It's not so simple. I want to belong here."

They said goodnight and didn't touch. They looked at each other and he turned away.

Two days later, after calling his parents – his dad had received the cuf-flinks and had locked them in the drawer next to his bed to keep them extra safe; his mom wanted to know whether she should send him vitamins – he phoned Kelly to ask if she wanted to meet for coffee. He didn't like cof-fee much, too bitter, but he wasn't sure what else to suggest for an afternoon meeting. She said she couldn't, because her boyfriend was there. But would he come for supper with them tonight?

"I'd like that," he said, feeling blue.

She ignored whatever might be discerned in his voice. "See you there."

"What can I bring?"

"Wine, if you like."

He went to Sainsbury's and bought an expensive bottle of red wine, sixteen pounds, with a distinguished-looking label. His scholarship would stretch to that, surely. He had been living frugally.

When the door of Kelly's place opened, there was a tall, slender blond man, with rosy cheeks. "I'm Ralph," he said pleasantly. "Nice wine. Excellent."

They sat down to eat after some chat that was, at least to him, stilted. In one of the silences he hummed, to give some aural texture to the stillness, but then Kelly asked him what he was humming, and the silence returned, thicker. He found that he liked Ralph, who was willing to talk about his mountain adventures and about new developments in computing – he hoped to get into technology after he grew tired of guiding tourists through the mountains – but Kelly was quiet, and her stillness disturbed the air among them.

"Let me put on some music," she said finally, and got up abruptly. They watched her as she went to the CD player and rummaged in the rack. "Top hits of the eighties," she said musingly.

The conversation went better when it was punctuated by pop. Their unease was countered by the upbeat melodies, and Kelly's quiet could more easily be set aside. After all, she was clearly not a garrulous person. She and Ralph went to the kitchen and emerged with three plates, each containing a tightly packed, deep green plant. For a moment it seemed as if they had hunted down and cooked some lush treasure of Eastern Cape fauna. But then Ralph said, "I bought some artichokes, so we thought, let's use them."

He had never seen an artichoke outside the Pick n Pay deli; certainly his mother had never cooked one. This proud, intricate plant was a different proposition from the pallid fronds that he had fished from oily glass jars, brought home as a treat. "You pull off the leaves and eat them," Kelly said.

He got stuck in. The leaves were indeed extremely chewy, with little flesh on them, a pocket of sweetness. He was already full by the time he'd gone once around his artichoke.

"Um," said Ralph. "You just take the bit of meat off each one. Then you throw the leaves away."

"No," he replied, with a sad sense of inevitability, anticipating that he was going to commit himself to a course of action that would make him look odd and hurt his stomach. "I like the leaves. I'm going to eat them all."

"You're crazy," said Ralph, watching him take another leaf and chew it up completely. This time, in his hurry, he swallowed a tough, stringy one before he had properly chewed it

"Is that the Smiths playing again?" he asked, to detract attention from his eating. "Sounds like those cheery guys."

"Good guess, definitely like them," said Ralph. "But no." The song permeated the flat, passing over the cutlery and the half-devoured artichokes.

"I like it, though," he replied. "I mean, it goes on and on, but the words are worth hearing on a loop, aren't they?" He appealed to Ralph. "'Where is the tenderness?' That's exactly right, isn't it?"

"Sure," Ralph said amiably.

"You're nearly at the heart," Kelly said. "The best part."

It came to him, in a perverse turn of mind, that after swallowing the leaves whole, perhaps he should refuse the centre.

"Eat the bloody heart," said Kelly, watching him with her half-smile. She seemed to know him.

"You want me to take this thing, all its protection gone bit by bit, and gnash it to a pulp?"

"Not if you feel sorry for it," she said, teasing again.

"I do, but that won't make a difference." His South African voice was back in full. He picked up the core of the artichoke. "Shame, man – sorry." Then he popped it into his mouth. He had eaten nearly every part of this object, even the indigestible outermost leaves, and was due his reward. He bit into the heart, the flesh soft and yielding.

Greg Lazarus is the pen name of husband-and-wife writing duo Greg Fried and Lisa Lazarus. Greg is a philosopher at the University of Cape Town. He teaches various topics, including the philosophy of mathematics and the history of philosophy. Currently Greg's research is in social choice theory, which deals with methods of reaching collective decisions. Lisa is a psychologist and freelance writer. She has Masters degrees in educational psychology and creative writing, and a higher diploma in education. She has written for publications including Men's Health, Femina, Shape, Cosmopolitan, Cape Town's Child, Psychologies, *and the* Mail & Guardian. *Lisa tutors Magazine Journalism, Feature Writing and Memoir Writing for SA Writers' College. The couple have co-written a memoir,* The Book of Jacob: A Journey into Parenthood *(Oshun, 2009), and a psychological thriller,* When in Broad Daylight I Open My Eyes *(Kwela, 2012).*

The House of the Apostate

Abdul-Malik Sibabalwe Oscar Masinyana

"Allahu Akbar," Minhaj said, and the men and boys behind him and the women and girls behind them mumbled the same and followed him down to prostrate their foreheads on the carpet. The carpet was Persian, and sat like skin on the natural stone floor, leaving unprotected only the edges close to the four walls – its deep red, sage green and black colouring subdued by years of sun and the sea breeze blowing off New False Bay.

"Subhana rabbi al-'Ala", he was whispering under his breath, "Subhana rabbi al-'Ala, Subhana rabbi al-'Ala", all the while thinking of the weather outside, how frustrating it was already but how much worse it was still to become. It was going to be another severe winter that's for sure – everyone knew that by now – and the first of the snows was definitely going to fall that night. Minhaj was also rather sad Ridwan couldn't be here this evening. It was the 15th day of Ramadan and Minhaj and Jaanaan had invited guests for iftar.

They were praying in the lounge, the most spacious room in the house. During the day, when its silk curtains were not drawn, it was also the brightest, flooded by a stream of natural light coming through the wooden-framed glass doors taking up the entire west wall. The doors led into a garden in autumnal neglect, but usually abundant with flowers surrounding the ivy-covered glass shed, once Jaanaan's studio, now packed to the brim with stacks of furniture. Beyond the garden was a fence wall and beyond the wall, the sea. The rumble of its waves was particularly loud this evening. Its movements always created fear in both Minaj and Jaanaan, who were still unaccustomed to its temperament and had never allowed themselves to trust it for too long. Kept awake some nights, Jaanaan said she was sure one day it would cover up the house and morning would find them all dead. Nine years ago there had been no sea near their house; and thirteen, perhaps fourteen, years ago winters never got this cold either. Then slowly, first in areas that were then close to the sea – Sea Point, Green Point, the CBD – thin layers of sleet began to grace the streets once a year. Then year by year, and with rising speed and ferocity, the whole landscape turned white for days and then for weeks and now for months from winter snow. The temperatures had become miserable. Miserable, miserable, miserable; no one was used to it at all.

No one except the children and Ridwan. The children because this was the world they grew up in and Ridwan, well, because Ridwan was Ridwan. Minhaj was visiting him at his old house when the first snowflakes fell. He had raised the palms of his hands to the sky and recited from the Qur'an, "Whatever is in the heavens and on earth, doth declare the Praises and Glory of Allah. To Him belongs dominion, and to Him belongs praise: and He has power over all things." At the moment when everybody was beginning to panic, Ridwan's heart was bursting with joy and thanking his Lord for the gift of snow. "I thought I'd die never having seen snow," he had said. So great and genuine was his excitement that he sprinted out to the street to examine the flakes as they fell all over him. Behind curtains neighbours laughed, but one by one the kids living in the houses on that street (now underwater) were allowed to join him, and soon even the adults were out and the whole street was filled with joy at the first sight of snow. It was beautiful then, because it was novel, and most people thought and hoped it was a passing anomaly. Other people, but not Ridwan; Ridwan celebrated with the full awareness that from now on this was how winter was going to be.

With salaah over, Minhaj instructed Ikhlas and another boy to lift the East Indian rosewood table to the centre and spread cushions around it. The boys bedecked the table with savoury foods Jaanaan had spent all day preparing and was now passing on to them from the kitchen. All the men took their positions around it, while on the carpet closer to the closed garden doors Amina laid out a cloth Jaanaan had chosen to demarcate the women's eating area. It too had cushions around it and was brimming with its own share of delicacies. Jaanaan also placed the electric heater by their corner. The older women, Hajji Fayiza and Hajji Rabi'a, mothers of Sulayman Wadud and Lubna Hakim, were brought chairs to sit on and Jaanaan insisted they wrap themselves in quilts she had dug out for them from her bedroom kist. Soup bowls with chicken and leek soup were circulated with freshly baked bread, and typical of Ramadan more "bismillah"s were heard around the room than it was customary as spoonfuls hit mouths again and again.

The soup was a welcome antidote to the chill, and the room was warming up from the lively conversation and the joy of food after another day of fasting. The men were talking loudly, laughing at Minhaj's anecdotes from his last business trip to one of his bank's overseas branches.

"How I wish I could go there again, but it's very unlikely," he concluded his narrative and this seemed to momentarily dampen their spirits. Overseas travel was now a luxury most of them could not afford, and was also an extremely difficult endeavour. With fewer planes legally allowed to operate, a trip now had to be booked at least six months in advance for any chance of leaving the country and it was extremely expensive.

At their eating place, the women, in hushed tones, were talking about Zakia's divorce from Samad.

"Apparently he sent her an SMS issuing her with one talaq," Hajji Fayiza confirmed.

"And she's had to go back to her family, like –" Lubna was trying to say something.

"*Men*!" Sufiya interjected.

"But at least they can still remarry then –" Aziza stated the obvious.

"Yes, alhamdulillah, but like –" Lubna's comments were often ignored for their whiff of gossip.

"Alhamdulillah, he did not issue her with all three talaqs," Aziza continued, as if to console everyone.

"That's beside the point," Sufiya was saying. "He probably thinks if he only issues the one then he can come back if things don't work out for *him*. He's just leaving himself a backdoor to come back in if his galavanting doesn't work out. That's just very unfair," the entire time her hands moving in sharp angles to reinforce her point. "*Men*!"

She's always having these strange ideas, this girl, the older women communicated their thoughts through shared glances, but were still too hungry to bother correcting her.

"Do you know how worried we are about Zakia? But I hear that when she –"

Benazir cut off Lubna and said, "Sufi, what are you doing tomorrow afternoon, yeah? Oh good. I need you to come over to my house, help me with something, yeah," and gave the other women a knowing smile. There was relief all round. Benazir always knew how best to deal with these things.

When eating was done and Amina and Ikhlas had cleared up the plates, Jaanaan and Lubna brought out desserts and offered everyone spiced tea and coffee. Many were grateful for the coffee, as most of these men and some of the women still had a long night of prayers ahead of them at the mosque. Minhaj had already decided he wasn't going for taraweeh tonight. Nor would he establish it in his house. This Ramadan he had attended only four night prayers and it was already halfway through the month. But that wasn't so bad, he reckoned, given that this was already an improvement from last year when he only went to three for the whole month. And perhaps it wasn't, given that Minhaj was in a serious spiritual crisis, so serious now that even his generally optimistic and self-forgiving instinct was starting to wonder if he could still consider himself a Muslim. After the guests had left, Minhaj only had energy to lie on the floor and stare at the mosaic on the left wall while he felt his food settle. It was a ridiculously large Moroccan mosaic they had brought from their honeymoon thirteen years previously, when they were still in their twenties and Jaanaan had just graduated from art school and he had already been working at the bank for three years. It was made up of a hundred square tiles inscribed with the ninety-nine names of Allah in ornate Arabic calligraphy. Looking at it now made him feel guilty. He turned his back to it and looked at the painting instead.

On the right wall, in dialogue or debate with the mosaic, was the only other mounted object in this house. It was a triptych Jaanaan had started painting a few months after their return from Hajj and completed almost two years later during her last days as an active artist shortly before the birth of their second and last child, Ikhlas. The painting – with its large field of burnt-orange earth, clouds of white and grey infused with streaks of dusk's orange, pink and red, interrupted with patches of blue sky over the solid black monolithic stone, itself sparkling with spots of gold – was the most colourful but also darkest object in the room, and it lent a dark hue to an otherwise bright and spacious lounge. The painting stimulated a chain of unsettling sensations in many onlookers, as if it was communicating far more than its surface appearance suggested, but was gagged by inexplicable forces operating beneath its carefully measured strokes. Although it had been hanging there since Jaanaan suddenly (and with unbelievably frantic energy) began to declutter the house and redo it almost entirely with her 'furniture sculptures' nine years ago, even Minhaj could never look at it for long without some inarticulable discomfort arising in his breast, and he had noted similar reactions in some of the men around the table when they threw glances at it every now and then.

He got up and went to bed while Jaanaan and Amina were busy clearing up in the kitchen. Minaj's crisis had been underway for a decade, but every Ramadan he would become particularly edgy; sleepless nights, restlessness, moving about so much that even Jaanaan always seemed to be awake. With the sea swoshing outside she would turn around in their bed, wondering what was wrong with him and Minhaj would say nothing. She would pretend to go back to sleep to leave him to his thoughts, though Minhaj was certain she was still awake, worrying about him. He was grateful to her for that, and for many other things. But he hated being the cause of so much worry and would not dare burden her with matters she could never guess, being so easy and contented a spirit. In the early days of his crisis, when she would catch him praying in the middle of the night with tears streaming down his face, she too would start crying with him, even before asking what was the matter. He would say, "I am thanking and praising Allah for all the goodness and mercy He has shown me and asking for more of His compassion," for how could he tell her what really troubled him? The only person he could possibly speak to was Ridwan, but even he, righteous as he was, Minhaj could never fully trust with his dilemma.

"You have been cursed by Allah." It was that comment that must have started this downward spiral. "Allah's curse has fallen on your household because of the haram work you both do," Imam Hassan had said, staring at the infant in Jaanaan's arms. "You need to ask for Allah's forgiveness and leave your lines of work otherwise He will continue cursing you." The whole community had been invited for the baby-naming ceremony and Minhaj had been so shocked by how angry he became even though he took this assault rather quietly. Jaanaan looked like she was about to cry or curse, but then stopped herself. It was Ridwan who defended their honour, reminding the imam that all life was precious, including the life of a little boy born with the special condition of an oversized head. Minaj, however, could not forget the imam's words, though he never discussed them afterwards with Jaanaan. He kept thinking about them, dwelt on them for so long that he lost his bearings. What was in his heart no longer echoed what was in his head nor did these resonate with what made up his soul so that his eyes would water and his body shiver at the mere recitation of an ayat from the Holy Qur'an as had been the case for years before. Even Ramadan, which in the past had served as his refueling station, now seemed unsuccessful in convincing his heart to tell his soul that it was now time for salaah, more especially now.

The doubt first showed itself in his disregard for small things, but then grew to encompass the abandonment of the big, fundamental principles. Long before he stopped saying bismillah before eating his meals, he had already stopped washing his hands before touching his food. Unless in company, he had even disregarded eating with his right hand and avoiding his left. He was no longer conscious of entering the bathroom with his left foot first and reciting the short prayer of protection against jinn and the demons residing there. All these sunnan matters had been pushed aside and, since the previous year, he had begun ignoring some of the days of Ramadan.

He always performed subh though. He could not skip the morning prayer without Jaanaan and the kids being aware of it. In the past he had forced Ikhlas to join him but now almost ten, the boy simply resisted him and Minhaj let him be. He felt he'd done his duty by him as a father, had taught him how to pray, and was not going to continue dragging him out of bed now that he knew what his Deen expected of him. Jaanaan rarely ever joined him and Minhaj preferred it that way. He had made them a massive fortune through his Islamification of capital investment stocks and bonds, and not needing to work, she rose an hour or more after he was gone and performed her morning prayers alone. However, since it was Ramadan it was impossible not to have the whole family pray together in the morning. So Jaanaan woke him up and also woke up Ikhlas and Amina, and while they performed ablution she prepared the pre-dawn breakfast meant to sustain them until sunset.

Halfway through his work day he prepared to go to mosque. He was already thirsty and was tempted to steal a glass of water but decided against it, worried his guilt would be written all over his face. Of course he still had a bit of his beard and donned his jalaba and fez for special gatherings as he did now for jumu'ah. Among his fellow congregates he enunciated his As-salaam alaikums, knew when to say Alhamdulillah and Inshallah and under the right circumstances, complained bitterly about the Jews and how impossible they made his work at the Islamic bank. He could also cue in an exclamation of horror upon hearing an account of some blasphemy such as the one Sulayman had just witnessed.

"Right there, in front of the mosque, was this giant billboard advertising next week's sexpo!"

"Astagfirullah!" Minhaj said.

"I couldn't believe it, the shamelessness! I told them I wasn't goin' nowhere until they moved it!"

"Mashallah!" Minhaj said in encouragement.

"'Nowhere,' I said to them! I said to them, 'You know that it's Ramadan, right?' and they didn't even know! I told them straight, 'I'm not goin' nowhere until you take down that filth!' and alhamdulillah, they did."

Although the emotional meaningfulness of such acts, phrases and robes had been sagging for years, Minhaj still believed he believed in Allah, loved Him still, a belief that had turned him adverse to the kind of khutbah Imam Hassan was giving, but to which he was listening with sustained attention for the first time in months.

"If you don't do your five salaahs, you're no longer a Muslim!" Imam Hassan was saying, repeating this endlessly, quoting from the Qur'an and hadith to support his point, and becoming firmer and firmer with each citation.

"During Ramadan shaytan is chained, so if you do bad deeds they all fall on your head because shaytan and his minions are not there to influence you."

After the Friday prayer, Minhaj went in search of Ridwan.

"Powerful khutba," Ridwan always said this as he shook Minhaj's hand and kissed his cheeks.

"Yes, alhamdulillah," Minhaj said, somewhat failing to sound cheerful this time.

"You seem troubled. How are Jaanaan, Ikhlas and Amina?"

"They are all well, alhamdulillah. You should come for iftar this weekend. Or if it's easier for you and Hajji Nazira we can come to you, and Jaanaan will help prepare the meal."

Ridwan waved his frail left hand, "Oh, we are old but we can still put together iftar for our guests! We're not barbarians! Besides, it's our barakah to serve you!" Ridwan said, still holding onto Minhaj's right hand and then covering their intertwined hands with his left, with Minhaj following suit. There was a bond there, a very strong one, which was affirmed one way or another each time these two men saw each other. Ridwan was one of the most respected men in the community. He had long taken a keen interest in Minhaj, and his wife Nazira had done the same in Jaanaan. Being themselves childless, they had sort of adopted the young couple and treated them as if they were their own children, supporting them in every way they could: giving advice, sharing suppers, babysitting their children, in everthing. In Ridwan and Nazira, Minhaj and Jaanaan knew they had at least two people who had their best interests at heart, and this feeling was mutual. It was hard now to imagine their lives without each other.

"Hajj, don't take this the wrong way, I don't mean to disagree with Imam Hassan–"

"But! There's a 'but' there, isn't there?" Ridwan laughed. That drawn out infectious laugh that made him such a companionable fellow even in his old age. Minhaj laughed with him.

"Yes, but…" Minhaj whispered, "Is it really acceptable to say that someone who's abandoned one or some of the principles of the Deen, in this case performing salaah, that they are no longer a Muslim? I mean, how can we know what's in their hearts? How can we be certain of their reasons?"

"Ah. I see."

"I mean," Minhaj felt the need to buttress his point, "Take zakah. Many Muslims don't pay zakah, even though it's enjoined upon them to give away that part of their wealth. But we don't go around condemning them to hellfire, do we? Isn't that a bit –"

"Hypocritical?"

Minhaj did not want to answer that as he felt that it was his behaviour, his very questioning, that was being questioned. Instead he added, "I mean, by Imam Hassan's standard the whole Muslim ummah wouldn't be regarded as Muslim, surely? There would be no ummah!"

Ridwan just smiled, put his left hand on Minhaj's shoulder and said, "Minhaj, you must always have a good opinion of us, your fellow brothers and sisters. You cannot comfort yourself with the assumption that we all have a pillar of Islam we're not implementing in our lives. You must presume the ummah's perfection at all times, but not be blind to you own imperfections."

Minhaj had a sinking feeling that even Ridwan would be unhelpful. That he too would issue him the same stock phrases that had failed to console him in his decade long drought. There was nothing left to do but nod and pretend to see the profundity of the response he would have expected from everyone else except Ridwan.

Still holding onto Minhaj's hand, Ridwan moved him away from the crowd towards the parking lot and began to say in an even more earnest tone, "I don't have an answer for you, Minhaj. Allah knows best, you should make dua to Him and read more Qur'an. Maybe His appointed scholars and teachers might know more, but I'm no teacher, just a seeker, like you."

He was serious, had the kind of face Minhaj had not seen on him since the last of his parents had died and Ridwan had told him about Allah's immense love for the orphan.

"But Allah has sent you to me for a reason and I feel obliged to try and be of some help. So I can tell you a story that I read once, long ago. A story that shocked me so much I never dared tell it to anyone else until now. I think you're ready to– . As-salaam alaykum," Ridwan greeted the people passing by to their cars, clearly not intending for anyone else to overhear this story. Minhaj could barely wait for the stream of passers-by to dwindle, but Ridwan seemed particularly sociable today. Perhaps he could see Minhaj's impatience and enjoyed his attempt to act as though he could wait for as long as necessary to hear the story he had been promised.

"Well... I was still telling you something, wasn't I?"

"Yes, a story that shocked you so much you –,"

"Ah, yes, yes, that's it," and he started walking in the direction of his car.

The rest of the afternoon at work was unproductive as Minhaj could think of nothing besides Ridwan's story. He forgot about his earlier thirst, only thinking *Oh Allah, what happened to that man?* He did not have his car with him, at least three days a week he walked or bussed to work – as the director of the bank he felt he needed to show solidarity with his workers, most of whose purses had been badly affected by the changing times – and so now he decided to walk home, despite the snow that had started falling after jumuah. *Did he go to jannah or jahannam?* was all he kept thinking.

"Every day for almost sixty years he climbed up the minaret to call others to prayer," Ridwan had told him. "Five times a day he would climb up and down and thereafter perform salaah, in congregation, even in his old age. Ah, it's going to snow soon," Ridwan had said walking slowly to his car, looking at the sky.

"Yes, the weather service said so," Minhaj had said.

"No Minhaj, you must learn to be the watcher of the times. That is our way. I can tell it will snow by looking at the sky. Anyway, on his deathbed, surrounded by a tide of all the faithful praying for him, that man renounced his Islamic faith moments before his last breath. Said he was doing it to save his soul!" Ridwan had paused and Minhaj thought he heard him chuckle. "Astagfirullah. He hadn't been a believer for over half a century. But there he was, every day, with all the trappings the very best of believers could possibly hope for, but disbelieving." Ridwan had paused again, this time for longer, as if to allow the story and its intended moral to sink in. Minhaj must have looked too bewildered, too taken aback by this story so that Ridwan immediately added, "Personally, I think that is what we should worry more about, the sincerity of our ummah, than whether people skip this or that or forget this or that. But astagfirullah, Allah knows best."

Minhaj only realised when he took off his shoes that the snow outside must have thickened since this morning. The house was very cold, and Jaanaan and the kids were out, but would be back within the hour for prayer and iftar. He could do with the silence, and these few moments alone in this house, with the sound of the waves beyond the garden wall, was just what he needed to resettle his thoughts. There was a lot of air in that house, breathing room, a discernable but disconcerting absence of clutter. Their house gave an impression of being a set of large empty halls scattered with carefully placed artistic objects, each of which attracted attention for its unique but unsettling craftsmanship. The house looked and felt bare, unlived in. There was a sense of being engulfed by space – or more precisely, by nothingness. Although it wasn't yet sunset, the sun had already disappeared by late morning, so he switched on the lights. Immediately, he noticed a note Jaanaan had left on the Indian rosewood lounge table, placed there so as not to be missed. It was in a bright silver envelope and practically glowed under the fluorescent lights.

In the early years of their marriage, they used to write each other letters, spontaneously, and leave them in prominently placed envelopes around the house. They were about all sorts of things, sweet nothings; how much she loved him still, how he brought her some more paint and put it in her studio, how she had completed a painting and he could now come and see it, how her painting was lovelier than the last, but that it was high time she made another sculpture and that in her studio was the very rare wood he had sourced for her on his business trip to India. The letters were like an alternative life they lived alongside their real one, and the two lives rarely coincided. Then he started being briefer and briefer in his responses, replied to fewer and fewer of them and eventually stopped entirely. Jaanaan never asked him what had happened, but accepted the ending of their game without any behavioural change in their practical day-to-day life. Anyway, all sorts of other things were changing then, in and outside of their house. Amina was two, running around like mad and causing havoc and Ikhlas was a real crybaby perhaps made worse by his condition and, truthfully, a strain on everyone. Shocking things were happening in Syria and in Egypt – and the rest of the Muslim world was in serious political turmoil. The markets crashed, the banks were blamed, he feared for his life stepping into the bank every day, with all those angry people outside, all insisting they were now homeless, poor or without pension because of the actions of banks and corporations. Meanwhile, the sea was reclaiming incredible amounts of land – Greenpoint, the city centre, Woodstock, parts of Observatory and Mowbray – literally stopping at their doorstep just before its tides receded again. Entire neighbourhoods gone, buried undersea in a matter of months. It was terrifying. They thought their house blessed, and in lighter moments Minhaj started calling it the Ark-Museum housing Nabi Musa's staff that conquered the Red Sea, something Jaanaan must have taken a bit too literally for shortly afterwards she replaced many items of furniture in the house with sculptures from her studio.

"You are turning the house into a museum," he had joked, and she had tartly told him that she did not want to be crushed by furniture in case of a flood, and Minhaj had felt the need to reassure her that the house was her domain and she could do whatever she thought would beautify it. Then one day, while in the garden, Minhaj had noticed that her studio was filled with furniture. She must have stopped painting or making sculptures and at first he thought it was because of the children, especially with Ikhlas's condition, so he hired extra help. But Jaanaan occupied herself trying out other things. She started a business making wooden children's toys, but did not get far with that. In time she got very far making clothes, amassed a lot of wealthy clients who could no longer get their expensive tastes catered for by the now slow imports, but eventually dropped that too. Said it wasn't stimulating enough. She fired all her help, saved all her money and devoted all her energy to running their house, tending to the garden and sleeping. So one day Minhaj decided he was going to keep on probing her until he received an answer that satisfied him.

"But how was seeing the Tate exhibition a reason for you to quit?" Ten years previously, they had been in London and visited an exhibition of Saloua Raouda Choucair's work, then touted as "perhaps the first abstract modern artist in Lebanon and even in the Arab world". Already in her nineties, her obscurity both within and outside of Lebanon would have been guaranteed were it not for that exhibition. Jaanaan, of course, had been fascinated by Choucair's work since art school and she was very excited about the whole thing, wouldn't stop talking about it, how momentous it was, though all the significance and the details were lost on Minhaj. Unless big money and the possibility of making an acquisition for the bank were involved, art bored him to no end. Yet on that occasion he did not object to visiting the gallery with her, he was particularly in love with Jaanaan around that time; maybe it was from knowing she was carrying their son or maybe it was just being on holiday in London.

Something about the work had unsettled her, Jaanaan now disclosed. Something she could not articulate until a few months later when she was trying to finish a painting she had begun almost two years before the London trip, the painting that now hung on the lounge wall. She realised, she said, that there was only so much she could do as a Muslim visual artist, given that she could only be responsive in a non-figurative language, only able to render observations of inanimate objects. The spirit of abstraction characteristic of the geometric principles of Arabic and Islamic art could only go so far for her. Eventually a point was reached beyond which nothing bold and striking could be produced, where everything collapsed into one thing, and it became a taxing labour to distinguish the uniqueness of one piece from another, let alone produce it. Approximately thirteen critically acclaimed paintings and thirty-three sculptures later she felt she had reached that point and could not continue anymore.

The answer had satisfied Minhaj, though something continued to bother him though he could never think about it long enough to formulate a proper follow-up question. So when the letters stopped, which were often about her paintings, Minhaj did not think much of it. Now, seeing this letter made him sad and guilty. Nine years had passed since her last letter, and now here was another, glowing in silver, and Minhaj was surprised at how excited he had become upon seeing it. He wanted to postpone opening it, desiring to savour the excitement that just seeing it had generated in him. Already he was feeling relieved. He had completely forgotten about Ridwan's story. The excitement overwhelmed him and he lunged for the envelope, opening it quickly but gently.

> *Minhaj,*
>
> *By the time you read this I'll be long gone, with a new name, a new life and a new religion. I can't continue like this anymore. I can't continue ruining your life and not living mine; I must live and to do that I must work. The only mahr I requested before our marriage was the studio you diligently built for me, among the flowers in the garden. I now return it to you as this is my way of divorcing you. I shan't be seeking Imam Hassan's approval on the matter; he won't grant it, I know it, so do you, and anyway it no longer matters. Tell them you issued me with three talaqs and I then ran off with a lover. That way you can re-marry and he'd be relieved to not have to deal with the shame. The signed legal papers are in the study.*
>
> *Do not look for me, Minhaj. You will not find me.*
>
> *The kids are with Hajji Nazira and Ridwan. I am leaving them with you with a heavy heart, a mother is not supposed to abandon her children. But if they come with me I cannot promise to raise them as Muslims and I know that would kill you more than my absence. So they are yours, and I know you will raise them well, I take comfort in that. I hope you will always know I love you. But I cannot continue like this anymore.*
>
> *May you be rightly guided. Pray the same for me. And for Amina and Ikhlas. Peace be with you.*
>
> *Jaanaan*

Minhaj suddenly felt very tired, remembered he was thirsty but grew very dizzy, pulled the closest cushion to his head and fell into a deep sleep, right there, on the carpeted floor.

Abdul-Malik Sibabalwe Oscar Masinyana is pursuing a Master's degree in Linguistics on the discourse marker ke *in Xhosa, and has an undergraduate degree in Film and Media Production, both from the University of Cape Town. He is a non-active director of Instika Agri-Media (http://intsika.org/), an agricultural media platform intended to support small scale farmers. His daily job involves fostering reading and writing communities in high schools, and he is the editor of the multilingual* Paperight Young Writers' Anthology. *He is working on his first novel, writes poetry and short stories, and once in a while composes an essay for his blog http://thebookofabuddingintellectualism. blogspot.com. If he has a mission in life it is to raise the status of South Africa's African languages for oral and written functions in every domain of society, particularly in agriculture, scholarship and public cultural life.*

Ponta do Ouro

Nick Mulgrew

"Let's hope being a bastard skips a generation."

Mum folds her glasses and puts them next to her tea.

"Your dad's grandfather was a bastard too, or so your gran told me. Always at the pub, smoking in the house, hitting his kids."

I sit up. "Dad's never hit me though," I say. "And he doesn't smoke."

"Doesn't he? I've heard different," Mum says. "You see, that's the thing. You think he's one thing and he's really another, like–"

"Wait," I interrupt. "Dad smokes?"

"Apparently." Mum sips her tea. "Quinton said he saw him having a cigarette at the George the other day."

"But he hates cigarettes."

"Apparently not." Mum drains her cup, "He's a bastard, son."

"Right," I say. I flick the kettle on again and pick out another pair of teabags: our almost-hourly ritual.

"And then this," she says, handing me a pile of paper. "Have you read it yet?"

It's a divorce summons, faxed to my mum earlier today – December 19th, her birthday.

"Great present, that," she says. "'Irreconcilable differences'. Yeah, right. He's got someone. I know it."

He does. But she doesn't actually know it.

It's been six months since my dad moved out. It would have been longer if it didn't take him leaving and returning a few times before he found the courage or the motivation or the desperation – whichever it was – to stay away.

Either way, it shocked me. I'd always thought my parents had a good marriage. At the very least I thought they were good foils: him, the dyslexic breadwinner; her, the warmhearted housewife who reads to school kids in Avoca Hills every week. But I found these things are rarely perfect. About a year ago he stormed into the house after work and told my mum he wanted to be single. No further explanation. He took his clothes and his golf clubs and left that evening.

Mum didn't take it too well. I moved back to Durban North from Glenwood for a week to see her. My dad came back the day I was supposed to leave, so I decided to stay a little longer. Dad was out again within a couple days, and then back in on his knees. Of course she forgave him.

This went on for a while until he signed a lease for a flat in Glenashley. I stopped going to lectures and instead took up drinking the beer he left in the fridge. Eventually I stopped paying rent on my flat. I permanently relocated to north of the Umgeni again, to the house I grew up in on Lonsdale Drive.

I avoid him now. It's easy for the most part: he's usually working in East London or stalking the pubs in Umhlanga village. Sometimes he'll force me to meet him for lunch at the mall in La Lucia, where I'll eat a wrap and chips and try to keep the conversation on football. Other times I'll catch him after rugby matches at King's Park, where he'll be braai-ing with his colleagues and their wives and daughters. Usually I'll pretend I've had too much to drink and that Yev is driving me home, just so that I don't have to drive him home myself. I'm still not used to seeing him stumble into Glenashley Heights, rather than the bedroom where he slept for the last 19 years of my life.

Not that I think he stays there full-time. Soon after he moved out he sent me an SMS that very obviously wasn't supposed to go to me. He didn't realise. I still need to tell Mum.

I'm sure I will, one day.

"Bastard," I say, trying to dispel the thought.

Mum takes our mugs to the sink and submerges them. She begins to sob. I go to put my arms around her. Her hands soak through the back of my shirt.

We're supposed to go to Mozambique in a few days. I'm not sure if we will still. Mum says she has to get litigation started, and stays on the phone all afternoon. I start on a six-pack of lager.

She had wanted us to go away for Christmas, to spend time together that wasn't overshadowed by my father's presence – or, you know, the lack thereof. She wanted to go to a place that she'd been to with her friends when she was much younger, a place she said where the world couldn't reach us. In her mind, a land of cheap rum, seafood and sunburn. A place called Ponta do Ouro, just over the border in Mozambique.

My friend Alex told me that it was a shithole – too full of Afrikaners – and that we should head further north to Praia do Tofo.

"She's ignorant," Mum had said. "She's too bloody used to Umhlanga. The beach is clean in Ponta. No sewerage, no Indian wifeys drowning in their saris. Clean. Peaceful."

I didn't particularly want to go, but when Mum brought it up it was the first time I had seen her excited since my dad left. So we booked a couple of nights at a place called Villa do Sol. It had looked alright online: wooden buildings, cane furniture with scratchy varnish, palm trees – the sort of coastal kitsch Mum takes to.

The next couple of days don't go so well. Mum holes herself up in her room with self-help books and hot toddies, coming outside only to cry or go to Mass. I bring her meals – cheese toasties and takeout from Nando's – and mugs of tea. The dishes pile up. I go through a case of beer. My dad's sisters keep phoning us. I unplug the phone.

And so I settle in for a Christmas, drunk, watching football. I buy trifle from Woolworths and another case of beer. They don't last long.

On the day before Christmas Eve I go to the Pauline Sisters in Overport to buy Mum a present. I settle on a small statue of Our Lady crying and cradling the baby Jesus. The sister at the shop says it represents both Our Lady's joy at the birth of the Lord, and her pain at her son's eventual death. I say that Our Lady didn't know Jesus would be crucified when he was born. She says I'm missing the point.

When I get home I ask Mum what she wants for Christmas lunch.

"Why?" she asks, sitting up in bed.

"So I can go to the shops and get a ham or something," I say.

"But we're going to Mozambique tomorrow."

"Are we?" I ask. "You don't seem like you're up for a trip."

"Nonsense," she protests, stuffing a tissue into her dressing gown pocket. "I wouldn't miss it for anything."

I try to dissuade her, admittedly more for my comfort than hers. She won't have it. She gets out of bed and rifles through her cupboard.

"Get packing," she says. "You'll need sunblock and Tabbard. I've got our passports. Oh, and start taking these." She tosses me a medicine container. Malaria pills.

"I'll be ready in the morning," she says.

She slams her door. I go pack.

"Red sky in the morning," Mum chimes.

"Shepherd's warning," I murmur. I'm hung-over. My own fault.

We pack the old Land Rover with our bags and head north. I feel dreary, but on the road I begin to feel better. There's something life-affirming about driving north, past Ballito, Mtunzini, Kwambonambi – but I can't help wonder what it is. Perhaps it's the exoticism, the feeling of traveling off a National road, deeper into the cane fields, away from signposts to Gauteng, toward places with much less pronounceable names.

Through KwaZulu the world gets greener, the potholes more difficult to navigate. Buses don't run past here too regularly, even in the holiday season. So people line the road up past Mtubatuba and Hluhluwe looking for a spare seat in a minibus or between the kids in a family sedan. Hitchhikers hold up cardboard signs scrawled with the abbreviated names of their desired destinations: "RB" for Richard's Bay, "UL" for Ulundi. Closer to the border they hold up R20 and R50 notes. Kindness is easier to find when it's remunerated up-front, I guess.

I pass them all by. "You can never trust hitchhikers, even the ones with babies," Mum says. "That's what they do, you know. They pretend they're rushing to get home and the next minute they have a gun to your head."

Getting to the border takes longer than I thought it would. Traffic sits stagnant along the one road through Kosi Bay. Black families fill the sidewalks with packets of chips and old suitcases. White families pour in with boats and four-wheelers on trailers, clogging up the petrol stations.

Eventually we find ourselves at the back of a twenty-car queue to the border post. We get out and shuffle to the immigration office. We only have to wait twenty minutes.

"Purpose of visit?" the official asks us.

"Holiday," I say.

Stamp. "Welcome to Mozambique."

A guard gives our car a cursory looking over before we cross the border. We go from tar to dirt road, from dirt to sand. A vague path here and there. A sign that warns about unexploded landmines lurking somewhere off-course – but what course?

Car hooters are indispensable here. Hoot every minute. Hoot before you traverse a hill, in case there's someone trying to do the same from the other side. Hoot before you take a blind bend. Hoot at the GP-plated car tossing spent cans of Castle out their sunroof.

"Smell the ocean," Mum says, rolling down her window.

"Smells the same as it does at home," I say.

"Stop being so negative," she says. "Look, it's beautiful!" She's right. It is: the pearlescent sand, the unsmogged sky. "We're going to have such a wonderful time out here, just you and I. A peaceful time. Somewhere where the world can't reach us."

A dune bike speeds past us just as I try to go over a hill. I hoot.

"Looks like the world will reach us just fine," I say.

"You're just like your bloody father sometimes," she snaps.

I stop the car. We sit in silence for a while, staring at the dunes. Sand blows against the windscreen in waves.

"I'm sorry," she says, eventually.

I start the car again. We go on.

Soon the coast turns leafy. We see settlements, huts, houses. Wooden stalls by the roadside sell green mangos, jars of peri-peri, and rum in plastic bottles: the essentials. The palms grow taller, the paths better-trodden.

A sign emerges in the distance. Mum sits up. "That wasn't there last time I was here," she says.

It's for a night club: "CARLITO'S – THE BEST JOL IN PONTA".

"The best *jol*?" I ask. "Don't they speak Portuguese here?"

I slow down. I crane my neck to look inside. Twenty or so sunglassed teenagers sit at picnic tables under canopies of palm fronds. Loud music spills out of unseen speakers.

"Grim," I say.

"Oh well," she says, "let's hope it hasn't all changed."

Closer to town, the sudden stench of petrol. Mum's lip curls as we enter. South African plates hang from every car. Insipidly-named bars – Casa de Praia, Angelo's Shack – open up onto the main road. A Bulls rugby flag flies over one restaurant. A market lines one side: more mangos, more chili, more rum. Clothing vendors sell MPLA shirts and slacks printed with the face of Nelson Mandela. Villagers eye us exhaustedly.

"Jesus Christ, Mum."

"Don't blaspheme."

Then, a clearing. Across a small field, a harlequin strip of tourist accommodation, restaurants and shops. Our hotel is one of them: a clump of shit-brown chalets with green roofs. We enter the parking lot. Out front there's a jungle gym infested with children. By the entrance to reception, a vervet monkey in a metre-high cage. A fanny-packed tourist has his camera pressed up close against the chicken-wire enclosure. The monkey swipes at the lens. The man jolts back.

We check in with a smiley local who carries our bags to the chalet. He kicks aside a broken flip-flop at the front door and dumps our bags inside. Out of breath, he asks us if we need any help with anything else. I ask him for a good place to eat prawns. Mum asks if there's a Catholic church nearby.

"Prawns, at Seamonga, just down the road," he says. "And church, just across there." He points to an egg-yolk yellow hall in the middle of the clearing.

"That's the church?" Mum asks.

"Yes, sure," he says.

"What time is Mass?" I ask.

"The priest, he usually comes at eight." He smiles. "But sometimes later. Just wait in the morning and he will come."

"Not the most assuring," Mum says. "Anyway, thanks." Mum gives the smiley man R10 for his trouble. At this I realize I never thought to exchange money.

"It's OK," the smiley man says. "Everyone accepts Rands here." How convenient.

We decide to go the beach for the rest of the afternoon. I change into shorts and slather myself in sun lotion. Mum comes outside with towels, and we head to the shore. Mum smiles – this, at least, hasn't changed: white sand for miles, a sea pulling azure and mild-mannered; the bay's shallow curves and its freckling of boulders and rocks and pools.

We head to the bay, where most of the beachgoers loll about. We pass sun-hatted men selling bags of prawns, bunched up like bananas. A gaggle of tween-age boys kick a rugby ball between them. It reminds me of someplace like home, dusted of its litter and black sand.

Mum stretches out her arms. "Glorious," she says. She grins freely, her skew teeth glinting in the sun.

We lay our towels out near the breakers. I kick off my sandals, lie down, and fall asleep. When Mum prods me awake some time later, I'm covered in sand.

"Get us a drink, would you?" she chirps.

I mumble, sundazed.

"A Coke would be nice," she says. "With some rum. When in Rome, you know."

I swipe the crust of sand off me and stumble toward the bay. There's a beach hut there. They should sell drinks.

A chubby boy, maybe ten years old, plays with a pair of scrawny white brothers outside the hut. They're throwing each other around on the sand, laughing while they pile on top of each other. The smaller of the boys is taking the brunt of it, but he seems OK. The fat boy's dad comes out the bar, shouting his name – "Fifico! Fifico!" He waddles inside. I follow and see him sitting on the bar top, chatting to some tourists. It seems his dad owns the place.

"You've gotten so big!" they say.

"Sim! Big!" Fifico says.

"His mother is a good chef!" his dad bellows, shaking his own belly in his hands.

I order a beer and a rum and Coke. Fifico heads back outside while his dad pours my drinks. I pay in Rands.

"Gooood," Fifico's dad purrs as I head out. "We like your money."

The boys are roughhousing again. They yelp and try to tug on each other's hair. Fifico trips the younger brother over again. He laughs at him and offers a hand up. But the boy thrashes out and pulls down Fifico's shorts. A man outside the bar points and jeers.

Fifico disappears into the waves, his shorts still around his ankles. His dad peeks out from the threshold holding a tray of drinks.

"What happened?" he shouts.

"That boy pulled your son's pants down," I say.

"Filho do puta." Son of a bitch. He drops the tray, hops onto the sand and treads out into the breakers. He picks his sopping child up and runs a hand through his hair. He stomps back to the bar, glaring at the brothers over his son's heaving shoulders. The two disappear inside.

I sip my beer. I leave.

Dark snatches hold quicker than we expect. We leave the beach after only a couple of hours more. Back at the chalet I shower in our shared bathroom. When I come out, Mum's reading her phone. She bites on her gums.

"Hey," I whisper, putting my arm around her, "What's the matter?"

"Nothing, pal," she says. She leans into my chest and takes off her glasses. "Your dad just messaged me."

"And what did he say?"

"Oh," she says, placing her phone face down on the bedside table. "Nothing. Just wishing us for Christmas."

"Anything else?"

"Nothing."

She twists her wedding ring around her finger. I think I know what she's thinking, but I know she won't say it.

We head out to Seamonga, the place the smiley man recommended for prawns. So we eat prawns, gigantic ones, ten or twenty each, drenched in butter and peri-peri. Mum tries to suck the gunk out of each of the prawns' heads, leaving a pile of soiled serviettes on the table.

"The head's the best bit," she says. I don't agree.

I want to mention Dad, ask where he might be spending Christmas, what he might be doing, who he'll spend it with. Mum probably knows as little as I do though.

Across the restaurant a young family shares a pot of mussels. "They look happy," Mum says, "Just like we were when you were young."

When I go to bed, I can hear Mum crying through the wall.

"Merry Christmas, darling."

Mum walks into my room carrying mugs of tea. She puts one down on the bedside table.

She kisses me on the forehead. "Come through when you're ready," she says.

I rise and open the blinds. It's overcast and still. I rummage in my bag for Mum's gift and bring it into her room. She's checking her phone, flicking through messages.

I give her the gift. I gulp my tea.

She peels the wrapping paper back. "Oh!" she cries, "It's beautiful." She kisses me on the cheek. "Thank you, darling. I love you."

"You're welcome," I say. "I thought it might cheer you up a little."

"Oh, it does," she says. She brings me my gift, a notebook with gold-leafed pages. I have two almost exactly like it at home. I thank her.

We sit on her bed for a while, sipping tea. This is not like last Christmas. This is not like any Christmas.

Mum drains her mug. "I think we should think about Mass," she says. "It'll be eight soon." She goes to shower.

I lie on the bed and watch the mosquitoes circle the room. At some point Dad tries to call me.

Outside the church the women chat in their pastel dresses. The men, rugged and skinny, shuffle around in crinkled chinos. Children play with toothpaste marbles on the verandah. The doors are locked, but no one seems to mind.

"Excuse me," Mum asks one of the men, "do you know when Mass starts?"

He shrugs and smiles. "Feliz Natal!" he says.

Mum smiles back. "I guess we'll wait," she says to me.

A procession of dirt bikes passes by. The air fills with the cough and chop of their engines. The churchgoers cluck their tongues.

But soon afterward an old Hilux bounds over the hill and into the clearing. A tiny, balding priest climbs out. "Feliz Natal!" he calls.

"Feliz Natal!" the congregation cries. They stand, uncreasing their clothes with their hands. Father strides across the lot, fumbling in his pockets for his keys.

Within a minute we're inside. We sit on plastic chairs. There are no pews, no kneelers. The altar is pine, draped with a thinning white cloth. No statues. No stations. No saints. The locals fill the left bank of chairs, the one closest to the lectern. We sit at the back.

After a moment's reflection, Father leads the congregation in a hymn. I can't understand it, so I concentrate on him instead: his sandals, his graying temples, his vestments stained with specks of oil.

He raises his hand and crosses us. "Em nome do Pai e do Filho e do Espírito Santo."

"Amen."

We follow the aerobics of Mass – the sitting, the restless standing, the hesitant genuflection. The first half hour passes in mutual unintelligibility, a game of mimicry between us and the congregation. The priest's words are slippery and spongy, twisting and falling over themselves. We respond in English, to the stares of the children. I follow the liturgy roughly: Penitence, Kyrie, Gloria, Psalms. The priest reads from the Gospel of João, proclaiming the coming of the Christ child.

"Alleluia, Alleluia!" we profess.

After the readings, Father turns toward the back of the hall and waves at us.

"You are understanding?" he asks.

"Yes," Mum says, sitting up straight. "We are, I think. I mean, Mass is the same everywhere, isn't it?"

"Yes, yes!" Father leans on his lectern. "I'm happy you are here," he says. "Even though this village is always full of tourists, we don't get many visitors in our church." He waves his hand over the rows of empty chairs in front of us. "So we like it when you come. Welcome."

"Well, thanks for having us," Mum says.

"Where are you from?" Father asks.

"Durban," I say.

"Ah, good!" he says. "I like it there. Big city!" He turns to the rest of the congregation and speaks. They wave to us. We wave back.

Father says a few words to the congregation, something in Portuguese. He speaks softly, like a grandfather talking to a child. Suddenly, however, he turns to us, his eyes big in his head.

"Now," he says, "I think in Durban you would have a sermon now?"

"Yes, Father," Mum says. "Usually."

"Good," he says. "In our church here, we don't have so many sermons. I don't like them. We are equal in the house of God, so I say here that we must listen to each other. I try not to speak too much. I let everyone else talk about the readings, the Gospel, you see, what it means to us."

"That's nice," Mum says.

Father steps down from his lectern and raises his hands toward us. "And as you are our visitors this Christmas, I think you should speak to us," he says.

"What?"

"Sorry, my English is not so good," Father says. "I said I think you–"

"Oh no, Father," Mum says. "I understood you. I just don't know why you would want to listen to us."

"You are our visitors," he says. "And we want you to share with us." Some of the congregation at the back start to shift their seats toward us. Mothers put their children on their laps. This is not like any Christmas.

"Now?" Mum asks.

Father steps away from his lectern. "Yes," the priest says, nodding furiously. "Now is good. You can speak and I will translate."

Mum looks at me. She knows I won't speak. And so she stands, under the gaze of the church. She shifts around on her feet, rolling the starts of words in her mouth.

"Hi," she stutters. "I suppose–"

She catches her breath.

"I suppose Christmas to me is about God coming down to earth and being like one of us." She waits for the priest to translate. "And that's important, because that means God is a person and it means we can think of him as a person. He isn't this big man up in the sky. He was once one of us, you know, living a human life with all of its pain. The priest translates. The congregation murmurs.

"But it's also about family," she continues. "Not only God's family, but our families. We should celebrate family on Christmas. It's about my family and spending time with them as God spent time with us on Earth. And for me it's important we're all together, me and my son" – I wave – "and, until this year, my husband."

At this her shoulders drop.

Father hesitates. "He is dead?"

"Oh! Oh no," Mum quavers. "We have just" – she searches for the right word – "separated."

"I am sorry to hear that," he says.

"It's OK," Mum says, but suddenly she collapses onto her chair. I reach for her hand. She pulls away and wails.

The locals edge their chairs back. The children shuffle on their mothers' laps, dropping marbles out their pockets. A couple land at my feet. I begin to pick them up, abandoning my hysterical mother to her tears.

Father speaks in Portuguese again. He tries to explain, I think. The congregation tuts sympathetically, I think.

I take the marbles back to the girl who dropped them.

"Go on," I say. "Take them." She doesn't move. I give them to her mother instead. She forces a smile.

I go back to my mother. I force my hand into her fist.

Father comes over to us. He squats next to my mother. "Are you OK?" he asks. She says nothing.

"Yes, Father," I say. "I'm sure we'll be fine. Just carry on with Mass."

He places his hand on my mother's shoulder. She looks up at him.

"Thank you," he says to her. He walks back to the altar.

Mum sniffs and leans onto my shoulder.

"I'm sorry," she whispers, finally.

"It's fine," I say.

Father raises the Eucharist.

"We'll be fine," Mum whispers.

"Hosanna in excelsis."

Outside the church, out in the clearing, there is a flag. There is no wind.

Nick Mulgrew was born in Durban, South Africa in 1990. He studied English and Journalism at Rhodes University, then at the University of Cape Town. He is an associate editor of literary magazine Prufrock, *a former contributing editor of the* Rhodes Journalism Review, *and has written for the* Mail & Guardian, Getaway, *and* GQ. *His poetry has also appeared in* New Contrast, Aerodrome *and* Carapace. *He lives in Cape Town.*

Mogadishu Maybe

Chukwuemeka Njoku

These flies again, they don't ever seem to tire from this chase. Big, bluish-green flies with thorns in their legs. They prick me anytime they perch on me, this is too much. Wham! I swipe at them with my right hand, this time I hit one. It buzzes off flying low; I think I caught its wing. Damn, which one is biting my ear? Another and another, God, this is too much, they are everywhere. They cluster around my ear, nose, mouth, even my eyes. *Get off me, do you want to blind me?*

This world is wicked to us, all of us. Me, my brothers and sisters, even to my friends. We are all suffering because of the sins committed by those people, the unbelievers. Our teacher says that the sins of the people in the city are the cause of this suffering, this acute dryness. We did not see the strangers here so why are we being punished too? Is it not the people that sin that God should punish? Oh, I remember, our teacher said we are being punished because we kept quiet and did not act when we should have. We should have gone to the city and fought the people there, even our people, those that have fallen away from the faith. They do not pray anymore, instead they party and drink alcohol as they wish. The women love men too much, they sleep with men that are not their husbands and nothing happens to them. They are sinful people like Alma. That one, when she was caught sleeping with a man, damn! She suffered that day.

I was returning from the market, my mum had sent me to go buy her millet. The donkey was slow as we returned; it could not walk fast. It does not really walk fast ever, but that day was the worst I had seen. Me, I had my turban wrapped around my head. I had bought it that same day, it was still new and white, not this brown thing that I have here now. It is a little longer than a year and it is this bad already. Rumpled and brown. I'm tired of washing it; Amina washed it the last time even though she was sick, that sister of mine, she is wonderful. As I approached the village I saw dust rise; it was the dust that alerted me. The road from the market is hilly and has many turns. Climbing the hill on the back of the donkey was not helping; I got down, leaving the bag of millet alone on it. The donkey followed me, turning its eyes like it had swallowed a big lump of grass. I hate looking at its ugly mouth. Its teeth are dirty, but not as dirty as some people's in the village. Those ones; flies follow them more than they do donkeys.

Instead of being dust from a whirlwind, I saw that it was caused by a commotion. People gathered as a woman flung herself on the ground, crying. There was much dust and noise, everything was chaotic. I climbed on the donkey, unsure of what to do or what might happen. I didn't want any nonsense. My mum would kill me if I failed to deliver the bag of millet. Cautiously I approached. The donkey was even more cautious than me. It stopped and looked away, turning its head this way and that without taking a single step forward.

"Bax! Idaa!" she screamed, rolling about violently in the dust as the lashes came down on her. Masculine hands kept beating down on her, their black bare feet kicking up dust as did the feet of the on-lookers. She folded herself at each hit and screamed. Turning and rolling in the dirt her hair covered in dust, she attempted to crawl away, but she was surrounded and the men did not stop. They kept on till her voice went faint and all I could hear was, "Joogso! Joogso!" Stop, stop. "Fadlan! Fadlan!" Please, please. The Chief asked everyone to stop and they did. The woman was dead. I was not shocked. She deserved it. Why did she sleep with a man that was not her husband? She had no reason at all to be with another man.

"Waa inaan duugnaa isada," someone said; we must bury her. They walked away, leaving a few boys and girls. Her mother ran to the spot, screaming and cursing the people that beat her child. "My child, my child," she cried. "May God punish all of you, all of you bastards." She held her daughter's head on her lap. I stood there watching, our donkey watched too. "Dhakhtar baab u baahannahey!" her mother screamed. We need a doctor.

Doctor? Why would one need a doctor for a dead girl? I thought. Then her hand moved. A cough followed, another, then blood gushed out of her mouth as she coughed more. Her skin was swollen and sore. She clung to her mother, her lips moving, but she said nothing. Her mother wept more, and I left, with the donkey carrying the bag on its back. That was a lesson to the others, all of them.

Today we woke up in the middle of this dry vastness of land filled with nothing but sand. We have been out for two days looking for food. We used to provide for ourselves, but now we cannot even drink water. No wells and no rain, everything is dry, even my mouth, it foams like our donkey's mouth when it used to be alive. We killed it one night when there was nothing for us to eat. My sister cried for days.

Food used to be sent to us from America, I think. We would go to the relief ground and queue up, all of us from Shabelle, men on one side, women on the other. When a wife got a food parcel, her husband would leave the queue, and when a man got food then the woman would leave the queue. No two family members went home with two different bags. The exceptions were for the chief and some soldiers. That was before the rebels invaded our village one evening and attacked the people that give out the food. They killed one white woman that night; Amina said she saw them do that.

They drove down in camouflage uniforms and shot straight into the queue of people, killing some people on the spot. They jumped down and caught some girls, especially the pretty ones. They took Amina. She screamed for my Daddy to help her. He heard and ran forward, holding a log of wood as he charged at the men. They shot him in the head. Three times, in the head; Amina saw it, then he fell and shook violently, and still they took Amina with some other girls and all of the food that was meant for us. The white men, the Americans, never brought food to our place again, instead they go far away now to Bakool. That is where we are headed.

The air is very dry, the wind is violent. It speeds past us, filled with sand, causing a really intolerable haze, we can barely see. If not for turbans, we would go blind, all of us. We walk on with turbans covering our faces. The sun is hot, the wind is tough and the flies are persistent. No respite, no rest, nothing. We are doomed, I can feel it. I get angry; many times I get angry at the townsmen, especially in the capital. I would kill any unbeliever, if that will make this suffering go away. The trees around here are stripped. They cannot shade a fly, let alone a human. My little sister is thirsty, she gasps for breath to cool her throat. I try it too; it only dries up my saliva. My mother brings her out of from her carrying cloth and puts her mouth to Nadifa's mouth, allowing her to take some liquid from her own mouth. Nadifa usually stays quiet for some time after this dummy refill; she thinks my mother always has water in her mouth.

Somewhere near a dry shrub I see wet ground, just that spot. It is urine. Maybe an animal did it, a dog or a pig. If it was still here we would kill it and eat it, even if it is a pig.

I kneel down and put my nose to the urine spot and inhale the smell of it. With my eyes closed it feels like I am in another world. The smell like that of dust, of clay, mixed in rain water, is pleasing.

The last time I remember the rains is more than a year ago, when Nadifa was born.

"Asad! Asad!" my mother calls. "What are you doing with your nose in the sand, have you gone mad?"

I get up and run towards them, they have moved far ahead of me. The wind pours a wave of sand into my face and I fall, shielding my face with my hand. I am injured on both knees and my palms. My knees are grazed. The stretch of land around me twists violently in the heat of the desert. The land has changed now that there is no water.

I stand and run to them and she looks at me in anger. "You are the first child, you need to act like a grown up."

"Raali ahow, Mama," I say. "Sorry, Mama." I feel bad, I hate making her angry; she is my mother and my father too.

As we walk down the dry terrain, we see small signs of life. People, thin, hungry with ribs sticking out like basket weavings, walking corpses all. Some children are so ugly and dry; no amount of food can make them human again. There is nothing for animals to live on, they have all died. There is a dead cow on the ground; half of it is rotten already. The head is still good but its teeth are showing, clenched like a smile. We walk on. There has to be something for us to eat. God, is it when we die that we will eat? I ate in my dream last night, it did not help at all. That kind of food is bad. My mother has told me spirits offer food in dreams. They use it to lure away children that they want to keep for themselves. I cannot afford to keep eating in my dreams any longer; I will be taken.

At the foot of a hill my Mother sees one of our neighbours from Shabelle. "Ghedi," she calls out to him, "What are you doing here?" He looks up and beckons her to come.

"Sit down all of you," he says. My mother lets Nadifa sit on the ground. I sit beside her, then Amina and my mother sit too. There are about seven people seated in a circle; five men and two women. Ghedi cuts a slice of the meat and holds it out to Nadifa, she turns away and tries to cry. My mother points to the water bottle they have on the ground, "Please let me give her some water."

"Oh, take," Ghedi says and gives the slice of meat to me. I share it with Amina.

The noise around the fire is getting louder as more people come. Ghedi pours out more water from a can into the bottle and passes it to my mother; she drinks and passes it to Amina. It feels good to be quenching the wicked thirst of so many days. Ghedi cuts good sizes of meat for us and we eat. We enjoy it, the feast. The sun has set and an evening breeze is blowing. Long shadows and the cool evening make it seem as though life is getting better again.

"How did you come upon this kill?" my mother asks Ghedi.

"Oh this? It was a dying cow. It was never going to survive."

"You and these people killed it?"

"Yes. We had to, everyone is hungry."

My mother nods and stays sitting.

At a distance I see some people, white people. "Americans!" I shout, pointing in their direction. "Mama! Let's go take our own bag of food from them now before they finish sharing it!" I do not wait for my mother's approval before I run towards them.

"Asad stop!" my mother shouts.

Ghedi adds, "Asad they are not giving food!"

I stop. One of the white men is urinating.

"Mother," I say, when I return to the group, "I saw one pissing. Where did he get water to drink?"

"The one in khaki?" Ghedi asks.

"Yes, but they are all in khaki."

"Which is it?" Ghedi asks. "The short one?"

"Yes."

"He has been pissing like that since morning," he said. "I have been following them all the way."

"What are they doing if they can't give us food?"

"One government man said they are from London."

"Are they not from America?" asks my mother.

"They are from America, but London is their place."

"Is London like their Mogadishu?" I ask Ghedi.

"Yes, it is their big town like Mogadishu."

The fire cracks as logs of wood burn a reddened glow into the evening. It appears that we are passing the night here. I think of London, of America, of Mogadishu.

I must reach there, starting from Mogadishu. I notice a woman carrying a child, crying, she looks weak. She cannot even cry. The child is thin and almost dead. The eyes shine in that big head of his which hardly has a hair on it, a bag of bones.

"Please," she cries, no tears coming out, her voice dry and barely audible. "Please, water! My child! My child is dying!"

"Bring the water quick!" Ghedi shouts. Someone runs through the crowd and brings the plastic can. It is almost empty. The woman puts the bottle to her child's mouth and he drinks hastily.

"Let's run to the Americans for some water before they leave!" Ghedi pulls me with him and we run towards them. I have the plastic can with me. That man Ghedi, he is a strong man. He runs like he is not old. He is also fearless. He brought Amina back to our house after two weeks at the rebels' camp. He had gone to Mogadishu to buy things before he ran into a gun battle between the government forces and the rebels. The rebels ran away and the girls in their custody ran out, that was when he saw Amina and brought her back to us. I like him, Ghedi.

As we approach the people, I see them, three white men, Americans, and one black man, a government man and soldiers. They have a big motor there, looking like a house.

Ghedi knocks on the body, "Gbim! Gbim!" One soldier opens the door and points a gun at him, shouting, "What are you looking for?"

"Water please, water!" Ghedi pleads.

"No water here, go back!"

"Please water, a child is dying and we need water for him."

The men all look at us with only their heads showing. They say something to the soldier and he asks Ghedi to give him the plastic can. After a while, they give us back the can filled with water and the black man says, "Come in the both of you."

Inside there is light, table, chairs and beds. Beds inside a motor! I cannot believe it. When we sit down they give us food. Rice, stew, fish and something that looks like the intestine of a fowl cut into short pieces. I eat and eat, but I remember my mother and Amina and everyone there, so I stop eating.

As we walk down back to the foot of the hill, to meet the rest of the people, I feel bad that I cannot take anything back to my mother and my sisters.

When we get back to the camp for the night, more people have gathered, there is no more meat on the fire, it is finished already. Only the fire remains. We put down the water. A lot of people, women with lean, dying children gather around the plastic can, but Ghedi puts them into a queue and starts pouring out the water for them one by one.

"Where's the first woman?" he asks.

"She's lying over there!" someone shouts, pointing to a tree.

"Will she not come for water?" Ghedi asks again.

"She is over there weeping. Her child is dead, but she is still carrying it."

Ghedi walks out of the queue towards the woman and I continue sharing out the water to the never-ending line of people. Ghedi sits with the woman.

I cannot tell my mother about the feast that Ghedi and I had. I feel bad about everything that has happened. I will tell her tomorrow and ask her not to be angry with me. Next time, even if it means using my shirt as a container, I must bring some food to my mother. This night, I just lie down close to my mother and Amina and Nadifa. Other people are lying down too, just a few men sit around the fire talking. The fire itself has dwindled. Tomorrow we continue our journey to Bakool, we must get some food to eat even if it means going to Mogadishu.

Chukwuemeka Njoku is a Nigerian born in the late 1970s, living in Lagos. He believes that writers, irrespective of style and genres, are the conscience of society, aside from being agents of positive change. He has a collection of unpublished stories and poems, some of which can be found at www.poetry.onlinenigeria.com. Njoku Chukwuemeka is a contributor to the open night readings of Independent Poets Concerns, a poetry group in Lagos.

Looking

Beverley Nambozo Nsengiyunva

.

I want to share my toothbrush with someone. I want to find my coffee mug beside someone else's laptop in the mornings. I want my birth date to be someone's password to their email account. A man who snores lightly. My soul mate.

FACEBOOK   Desire Tobé

Whatshisname wants to be your friend

Do you know him?

What is on your mind?

Looking for my Soul mate
It's got to be a man.

3 Likes   2 Comments

I have hardly finished updating my Facebook status and already I have two comments with more coming in.

> Ben
> Desire, what's going on? Are you ok? Or is this another attention-seeking gimmick?

Ben has always been insensitive. He's definitely not the one.

> Ralph
> Hey Dez, check your inbox. Love you.

Ralph stands a chance.

It's midnight and we've just entered Friday 1 May, International Labour Day. More people will be able to read and respond since it's a public holiday. This year I promised myself that by June I should be with someone who I can talk to about my love for chocolate and turkey without being told off about calories. I need someone who I can talk to about my distaste for Ugandan women who always give me the malevolent look when they see me anywhere with Tom, my mzungu-Ugandan neighbour. A soul mate who will swim laps with me and not care that my bikini is disappearing under the flabbiness. The kind of person who will join me in pouring kerosene on the ants that find their way into my bathroom. Outside, I can hear the stray cats scrimmage for the fish bones in the cans. They overturn one of them and screech into the night.

Miaaaaaaaaaaaaaaaaaaaaaaaow!

I wait as they scramble over the upturned cans; I hear them knock against my car, an old green-lemon Volvo. It was my dad's. Now he has a driver, my mum. They're soul mates.

I feel guilty that the famished cats have to scavenge for food from the recycle bins. Between my flat mates and I, we can feed a hundred cats a week and turn their famine into fortune. I think that Gareth, Tom's cat, has grabbed the last piece of fish from the rubbish and managed to slide back into the building. Tom says that Gareth always picks the electricity bills from the gate for him and he also licks the dirt off his shoes when he returns from work. I know that Tom has a driver and hardly ever has dirt on his shoes. Many people have questioned why Uganda Revenue Authority would hire a mzungu but Tom is a fourth generation Ugandan. He speaks Luganda, Lumasaaba and Atesot fluently. Gareth has never licked my shoes but he always rubs against my leg until I throw him a biscuit or slice of bread.

Pauline Nambafu

Sis, you can have my bro if you're looking for a soul mate.

PaskaRegina

What is a soul mate?

TomTom
Dez, are you still up?

Desire Tobé
Yup

TomTom
Coming over, put some coffee on.

From my third floor apartment window I can also see the planes taking off from Entebbe Airport. From this distance I would like to believe that the entire country is lit up with working street lamps and that all the aeroplanes I see actually belong to our nation and not to Kenya or South Africa. It is rare that the planes fly over our apartment. The airport is streaming with people in that in-between state. They are in-between here and there but not yet quite here or there. They leave their destinies in the hands of a stamp. At my workplace, at Entebbe Registration Services, I see millions of names every day; receive data of new births and deaths by the minute. The entire population is in my hands.

I bought binoculars the other day from my friend, Landi, who was leaving the country for good. She told me that binoculars helped her to see things that she normally wouldn't have. Landi would say all kinds of things: "Did you know that most people in Uganda describe their relationship status as complicated? It's true. I was on the balcony at a Chinese restaurant looking down at couples on Valentine's Day last year and there were eleven couples on their phones. Nine of the women and six of the men described their relationship status as complicated and one woman said she was in an open relationship. Binoculars enable you to see such tiny details from far away."

I really miss Landi and her useless facts. I have only used her binoculars twice. The first time when I was looking for the tiny diamond that fell from my earring, and the other time when I was looking at a group of Marine Rugby players who were taking a jog around Entebbe. What a feast for soul mate-searching eyes that was! Thirteen sturdy men with thighs the shape and thickness of a pawpaw. Thirteen bronze and black chests. That moment took me to Heaven. Those men could have been the twelve disciples with Jesus at The Last Supper. They were delicious.

Tom is taking very long to come so I check my Facebook page again.

OLOWO

Babe, are you good? Holla!

SEBUTALE

May the God of Abraham and Isaac lead you to your true destiny and find you a soul mate straight from the throne room of the Lord's feet.

INDIFFERENCE

Yawn

33 Likes   14 comments

I walk across to the kitchen to make coffee. Tom takes his decaffeinated. Apparently Gareth's mother died after taking a saucer of iced coffee. She could only take decaffeinated according to the vet and so she died. I don't question the relationship Tom has with his cat. I do think it's weird that a man would allow his cat to lick the water off his body after a shower and that they would take cereal from the same bowl, but Tom is my friend, my best friend on the entire block. Coffee with Tom after midnight means two things. There will be less coffee and a lot of sex. If not that, then serious talk and a lot of sex. Either way, the bed is primped and pillowed. The duvet is folded at an angle for when we finally make it to the bedroom. The kitchen tabletop is clutter free and the light to the living room is off. It is not casual sex because there is no such thing. It is meaningful.

It all began when Tom brought me home in the pouring rain and my plastic Sandak shoes from Bata shoe store became unbearable. He offered me something warm, which was also the first time I actually ventured into his apartment. Usually, we met at the parking lot or just talked in the corridor. I went in and the cushion collection wowed me. He assured me he was not gay and was just storing them for his sister, who lives and works in Jinja town, where his grandparents own stores. We talked about our lives and he told me about his family who were born in Uganda. When he started explaining different Luganda proverbs as if to prove his story, I almost left because I felt he was showing off. However, I somehow ended up on the pile of cushions and then, after a moment, I was right at the bottom. We didn't intend to have sex. I told him I was a virgin and he told me that while virginity is noble, there are moments when we drift to a place of adventure that should be embraced. This was the place.

My mind at that point drifted to my dream of a white wedding and of my body meeting with a man's for the first time. The look of pride on my husband's face knowing that I kept myself for him alone. And then, two years after that we would have twins and move to Cape Town. It was all planned out. I knew that I had to wait. My friends in church told me that waiting was the best and only gift we could give to our husbands. How could I not wait?

Tom stepped closer to me.

"Desire, sex is not meant for an appointed time. It is perfect in its spontaneity with two consenting adults; the unexpectedness of its thrill is what sex is about."

Holding my hands, he gently guided me to sit down by the cushions. "I'm going to kiss you. If you don't like it, let me know. I don't want to force you to do anything."

When Tom said these words, my heart was beating so hard and when he kissed my neck, it was like swimming in caramel. I closed my eyes and did not want him to stop. I breathed heavily. I may have even moaned. I wanted this to go on for as long as possible. I did not remember how we ended up lying next to each other, naked, but when I saw how swollen he was and how big, I felt I should leave. Did he think I was going to allow that standing tree trunk inside of me? He had said I should say stop. So why didn't I?

The sex was excruciating because I was tense. My hymen took several thrusts before it broke and by that time I was begging him to stop. He was patient and impatient at the same time. He would stop to look at me and stroke my face, but I could not face him and then he would accelerate his thrusts. Something inside of me snapped along with the hymen. It was like a bolted door that had suddenly been wrenched open.

Tom taught me how to become better at sex and we never treated our misadventures as casual. We were truly committed and non-exclusive. I understood when Tom brought company over and he respected me, although I never slept with anyone else. This is why I know that it is the perfect time to find that soul mate. Tom's appetite does not make him qualify, however much I wish it. He is happy with many partners and I want just the one.

"Door's open," I yell from the kitchen.

He walks in with his cat in tow.

"Hey babe," he kisses my right cheek before forcing my lips open.

"I'll be here for as long as you need me before your soul mate arrives, you know that, right?" he says.

I place a saucer brimming with milk on the floor for Gareth. Tom downs his coffee and gives his cat a few fish bones.

"I'm sorry I couldn't leave him behind," Tom says.

"That's ok, as long as he stays in his place," I respond, while undoing the knot of my nightgown.

"Let me help you," he offers, deftly untying the knot and sliding the gown from my shoulders.

I guide his hands behind my back. I am wordless. I am waiting.

Tom wets my neck with his ravenous tongue before lifting me on top of the kitchen table.

"Tom, I'm sorry. I can't do this now. I need to talk."

He stands up straight and looks at me with a crooked smile. I know he is disappointed.

"Do you want to talk about that soul mate? I told you they don't exist. The moment you think you have found the right man, he'll be very kind to you in the beginning. He'll tell you all the things you want to hear and how you are so pretty and how he thinks about you all day. He will fill your inbox with poetry and descriptions that will make you walk around with a constant smile. You will be checking your Facebook status all day to see if he has posted a love quote on your time line and then you know what? He will suddenly drop you. After he has got what he wants, he will drop you. The five emails a day will reduce to five emails in five years. He will hide a camera in your room during sex and post videos onto YouTube and you will never recover from that embarrassment. Soul mates don't exist. I told you this before."

I stare at Tom as he goes on and on. His insight is not new. I know there is a little sense in what he says, but I also know what I want.

Reaching for my phone in the tiny basket of house keys just above the cutlery, I let Tom rest his head on my lap while I position myself more comfortably on the table.

RALPH
Have you checked your inbox yet?

AUNTIE MARGARET
I thought you had a boyfriend.

NANKYA
Soul mates don't exist. It's been proven. According to research conducted by the Institute of Anthropology at the Margaret Ann College of Humanities, soul mates are a figment of a certain part of our cerebrum that rejects aspects of human nature. 70% more women than… SEE MORE

I watch Tom saunter off and Gareth follows, giving me a grin as if to say it's time to take his friend back home. The sweetness of cold coffee settles at the bottom of my stomach like a puddle. It always feels like that when I'm hungry.

It's a quarter to two. Gareth rubs against my ankle as I rummage in the fridge for some turkey leftovers from a party at work. My boss made the turkey and nobody else wanted to take it home for the weekend. We were all told to bring some food. I took a chocolate cake which I had bought from the store since the power had gone off that night.

Gareth sits with his bushy tail tucked beneath him as he takes down each morsel of the turkey. I am reminded of the cats outside and wrap the last piece in a plastic bag. Wrapping my gown loosely over my frame, I push the door open and Gareth's furry frame brushes against me down the stairs to the parking lot. I follow him out of curiosity.

He carries his last piece of turkey down the stairs to the lot, where he finally drops it to the ground. At that moment two other scrawny cats shoot from the other side of the street with their own skeletons of fish and shreds of a pasta meal. Each of the cats drops their abundance at Gareth's feet. Their eyes, lustrous in the dark, stare fondly back at me after I drop my turkey beside them. I am intrigued. None of them scurries for the food as they usually do. It is almost as if they are waiting to say grace.

I am amused at their etiquette; wonder why I have never noticed it before. I am moved by their togetherness, united in feasting. A few scowls towards my right make me tilt my head in that direction. There are others coming to join this assembly. Two large black-and-white cats and a brown lean one. Unbelievable. It is carrying a piece of steak. Must be leftovers from the restaurant nearby. One of the black-and-white cats is wearing a half-empty milk packet on his collar. Someone must have tied it there. This cat peers at me. I diligently remove the packet of milk and return it to the small party. I need my camera. Tom beats me to it. He has appeared wearing only shorts and sandals and snaps away at the furry army.

"Dez, are these your friends?" he says.

"You know what, they just may be." I say. "But I've never seen anything like it."

Tom snaps away using his phone while I marvel. The cats are deliberate with their movements. They chew simultaneously. Neither of them steals from the other.

"Let's go inside, Dez," Tom whispers in my ear.

His lips are cold. I wrap the gown tighter around my body and wonder if Tom's hairs are enough to keep him warm.

"Let's stay a bit longer and watch this, or are you freezing?" I ask.

"I am feeling cold because you'd rather watch kitties eating than be with me," he teases.

"This is the first time that I have not seen them fight for food or howl at each other," I say.

"I know. Even Gareth is behaving. Let's take a walk," Tom says.

"In the cold?" I ask.

"It won't be so cold by the time we are done."

There are not many houses on the street. Some are so high and overlook the lake perfectly, while others are flat bungalows built in the style of Arabs and Indians. Our block of flats is the only one in the neighbourhood. Entebbe will always be the cleanest city in Uganda, with fresh air from Lake Victoria as well. A huge gust makes me shiver and Tom holds me tighter, leading me to a familiar road between two immense water tanks. We find our way to a park where Tom once held a barbeque for the community and he ended up with vultures attacking our meat. It was a good day nevertheless.

"I want to show you something," he says.

"I haven't been this side since the barbeque," I remind him.

"I know. Okay, we're almost there."

A little further ahead I see glow bugs filling the night air.

"Is this what you wanted me to see?" I ask.

"Patience."

And then I see it. In the direction of the airport, a little ahead, tiny reflectors appear to bob up and down on Lake Victoria.

"Isn't that the lake? It looks gorgeous."

Yes," said Tom. "Yesterday they finally finished the lights near the Travellers' Inn. The best part is that they allow visitors at any time of day or night for the first week. It was opened today."

"I thought it would be months before they were done. So, do you want to swim, in this cold?" I ask.

"Yes, after you of course," he laughs.

There are two cars parked outside the large bamboo tent which houses the Travellers' Inn. My legs are soaked from the dew and I am suddenly famished.

"Tom, you're half-naked and I'm in a gown. Crazy, much!" I exclaim.

"Not crazy, just adventurous, seizing the day."

"Or seizing the night."

We arrive at the porch and two couples are bent over a few beers and ground-nuts. They look up and one of them pulls two chairs for us to join them.

"Are you from this place?" one asks.

"Well, yes, we live in the flats about ten minutes from here. I'm Tom by the way and this is my friend Desire. We came for a swim and a walk."

"Hi, Tom and Desire," they greet while holding out their hands.

"I'm the owner's brother, I live in Nairobi and I've come to visit," says the bolder of the men.

I am suddenly extremely cold and the man asks if we would like anything. It is so cold and I need some tea. I take sips of the herbal rooibos tea while listening to the murmurs from the waves. Tom doesn't drink anything, reminding me of why we have come.

"Do you two need a room? We've got one upstairs," says the owner's brother.

"No, we're fine, just wondering if this swim will take place."

"Okay." I relent, "Let's just sit on the edge and dip our feet in, take photos, post on Facebook and that's it."

"Fine."

The ladies giggle, sounding rather ominous in the night. I keep reminding myself that it is after 3 a.m. and I am at the edge of the lake. Seize the day. Seize the day.

We gratefully take the large blanket that they throw at us and sit at the edge of a wooden platform. Tom leaves his phone on the table. I am reluctant to dip my feet in the water and wait as Tom does so first. He helps lift my feet off the edge. My toes touch the icy wetness. It is hardly refreshing, but the chill makes me feel like I am a part of this night. Tom wraps the blanket around us and covers our heads so that no one else can see us. Our cheeks touch and I lift my right leg over his left.

"Do you feel warm now?" he asks.

His left eye and my right one are blinking together like they belong to the same face. I grasp his hand that is squeezing my thigh. I can hear the soft splashes of the waves. I can also hear his breathing. I feel the hyacinth that has gathered at the edge of the water. I feel his body.

"Dez, are you still bent on looking for a soul mate?"

Tom gets so horny sometimes. I reach for my phone again.

> Katerine has invited you to like her page, **Soul mates of the World.**

> HAMED
>
> May you find your soul mate. Insha Allah

> JAY Z'S BRO
>
> OMG. TGIF!!!
>
> 41 Likes   22 comments

I don't even know how my hand slides into his pants, but Tom is as hard as the platform we are sitting on. Swollen like Tilapia fish. I hear him whimper. I put my other hand in his mouth and he bites it gently. His tongue tickles the tip of my fingers.

"Sit on me," Tom begs, throwing off the blanket.

Since we're already here after 3 a.m., might as well let Tom have his way. If my soul mate exists he will wait, won't he?

There is only one other person left at the table with half a dozen empty beer bottles in front of him. I sit astride Tom with my hands tight around his neck before parting his lips with mine. He holds my back firmly. I have known this tongue a few times now, never at the edge of the lake though. His touch warms me.

"Let's go up to the room," I whisper to him.

"Why, when we have this place to ourselves?" he says.

And then we hear the familiar miaaaow of a cat. It's Gareth. He has followed us all the way to the inn. He looks at us as if waiting for Tom to do something. He hoists himself so that he can lay flat with his legs out of the water. I hold onto his shorts and do not realize I am in the water until I feel my legs kicking frantically. My gown is billowing about. Stunned, the wet blackness engulfs me. Water enters my nose making me splutter. My arms flail. I have forgotten how to swim. I have forgotten how to keep afloat. I can't breathe. I can't breathe. I'm drifting away.

"It's so cold. It's so cold. Get me out."

Tom jumps in and, with his left arm around my neck, steers me towards safety. The drunk man by this time is kneeling by the edge of the water and holds out his hand to help us out.

"Are you okay?" he asks, offering me a towel.

"Let me get you some anti-bilharzia tablets, another blanket and tea. In the meantime, you can take off your clothes and wear one of the woolen robes in the cupboard. They are for visitors; you'll see them above the lockers. Take a warm shower both of you while I get the tea ready," he says.

I am moved by his kindness and directness. With my teeth chattering, Tom and I go upstairs as directed and I shove him away when he tries to join me in the shower. It is his love for adventure that brought me here in the first place. If he wants, he can share the shower with Gareth, not me.

"Sorry, Dez."

The hot water pellets are a relief and I don't stop until the room is filled with steam. I take the chance to write a few words on the mirror from the condensed heat, with my index finger before letting Tom in. I write, *Not searching for a soul mate.*

Beverley Nambozo Nsengiyunva is a Ugandan writer and poet who also acts once in a while. She has a Master's degree in Creative Writing from Lancaster University, is the founder of the annual BN Poetry award and devotes a lot of time to being a stay-at-home mum. Beverley was also shortlisted for the 2013 Poetry Foundation Ghana prize. She was part of a theatre-poetry hybrid project which she co-wrote with Ugandan playwright Judith Adong, featured as 45th New Plays Reading Series at the NYC, National Black Theater, in September 2013. You can read more about Beverley on her blog, http://walking-diplomat.blogspot.com, and website, www.bnpoetryaward.co.ug.

On Time

Achiro Patricia Olwoch

Achola is seated by a small swamp. This is no ordinary swamp; it has come about during a period of two weeks of non-stop rain which has flooded the land below the village where Achola lives. There are lots of flies around her because this swamp also has all the faeces and garbage from the village. It is a dumping ground. Achola does not seem to mind about the filth around her and she is not bothered when a house fly rests on her nose. She just chases it with a wave of her hand.

The truth is that Achola's village is not a village anymore. It is a camp – a simple collection of small makeshift huts in a large open area. The occupants like to call it their village though, because it is the only home that they now know. Each hut houses a family and is so small that a grown man cannot stand in it. There is one communal bathroom in the middle of the camp that serves almost thirty households, with latrines filling up faster than they can be dug. There is no room to fit a bed and each hut can only fit two small mattresses on the floor. The hut is the living-, dining- and bedroom all in one. Most of the time the occupants are forced to eat outside their huts because of the lack of space inside. There are hundreds of these little huts with only about twenty centimetres between one hut and the next. The children hardly have space to play and make do with the open spaces near the boreholes and feeding area.

Achola can see the trucks at a distance and she stands up to get a better look. She thinks that she is seeing badly when they disappear behind a hill. Achola shakes her head and sits back down. "It must be a dream," she tells herself. Just as she is starting to believe that, the trucks appear and this time they are clear. Achola claps her hands. They are the food relief trucks heading towards her village. She has to hurry and tell her mother. Achola has to be early to be among the first people in the line. That is the only way that she can guarantee that she will get some food.

"My child is everything alright?" her mother asks weakly.

"The trucks have come, Mama, I want to be the first in line," Achola replies without looking at her mother.

"Do not forget to take the right papers," her mother says, gathering as much energy as she can so that she can sit up.

Achola turns and sees her struggle.

"No Mama," she says, but her mother insists and sits up.

She looks at Achola and has a serious look on her face. Under the dim light in the hut her mother says, "You cannot fail. If you do, we will die."

Life has not always been like this for Achola. She has not always been seated beside a swamp covered with flies and she has not always been hungry and waiting for the relief trucks to bring food. In fact, it is not just Achola but the other people in the village as well. They have not always been sad and hungry. Begging and dependence are things that they were not used to in the past. They used to be a hard-working and peaceful people. Achola remembers living with her mother, father and three brothers in the village at the edge of the forest. They were one happy family and they never lacked anything. They had a whole home-stead with three big huts and a little one in the centre. That was their granary and Achola remembers that it was always full of food. Her mother and father and two older brothers always worked really hard each time that they went to the shamba. Achola always stayed at home with another one of her brothers who was supposed to look after her. He was only seven years old and she was four. Their mother always left them enough food and water to last until she got back from the shamba. Their village was very safe, so there was no worry of anyone hurting or stealing the young children.

Achola's father was the chief of the village and he loved his people. He was a wise leader and a good organizer. He introduced his village to the idea of saving up their money and crops for a rainy day. It was normal for every compound to have food in the granary, but he wanted them to have food that they would have over and above that. Thus he encouraged them to plant more crops than usual, and when they were harvested he asked them to keep more food away for the dry season than they put in the granary for everyday use. When they sold their crops, he encouraged them to open up accounts in the local bank in the town so that they could save up their money. Not many people opted for this because the town was quite a distance from the bank. They preferred to keep their money some place safe in their homesteads; like a small money granary.

The best part of everything in her village was when there was a celebratory feast. There was always lots of food to eat and all the village came together to celebrate. Parties were always fun. The people were spoilt for choice as to where to go. Whether it was the birth of a child or a wedding party, the celebration was just as big and just as nice. There were sad times too, like when someone died. People cried and everyone was very unhappy. There was still a lot to eat, but the mood was not as nice. Achola remembers all these things like they have happened the day before.

It was late in the night and they awoke to the sound of gun shots. People were screaming and there were lots of huts on fire. Achola and her brothers woke up and ran into their parents' hut.

"Mama, what is happening?" a frightened Achola asked as she ran into her mother's arms.

Her brothers were also terrified and they ran to where their mother was. Their father started to dress quickly. He wanted to go and find out what was happening to his village.

"Please be careful," her mother said, as she held their children in her arms. They all huddled together to wait.

Just as he reached the door, her father heard footsteps and he stepped back towards his family and closed the door behind him. Not too long afterwards there was a loud bang on the door. The person on the other side was ordering them to open it. The chief stood back and gestured to his family to be quiet. He hoped that these intruders would leave. Instead the banging got louder, until they finally kicked the door in. A man came rushing in and he had a gun which he pointed at them. He ordered the chief to step outside. When the chief would not budge, the man turned to point the gun at Achola, her mother and brothers. He again insisted that the chief get out or he would kill him and his whole family. There were other men who entered and soon the whole hut was full of these violent strangers. They wore the same colour army uniform and had identical scarves and bandanas tied across their foreheads instead of army caps. Most of them had dreadlocks.

Achola saw her father stand in front of the man and his gun as he tried to shield his family.

"Who are you people and what do you want?" he demanded to know.

"I am the one asking questions here!" the man shouted back at him.

As calmly as he could, her Father continued to ask, "What is the meaning of all this?"

"Enough! Get out, NOW!" the man shouted even louder. He was getting angry and he started walking toward her father as if to hit him with his gun. Achola's eldest brother ran forward to protect his father from harm. The man with the gun hit her brother on his head and he fell screaming onto the floor. He had a deep cut on his head. He writhed for a while and then he closed his eyes slowly as he breathed his last. He was dead. There was a scuffle as her father ran to his dead son's side. Her mother set Achola aside as fast as she could and ran towards her husband and son. The man with the gun then hit her father in the stomach and he fell over. Achola and her remaining two brothers stayed still and huddled together in the corner. If the wall could open up, they would have entered it. Achola closed her eyes. She thought that maybe if she did not see anything then it was not really happening.

"My child… you have killed my child," she heard her mother wailing.

There was another loud gunshot. One of the men had shot into the roof to silence them. Her father was then dragged outside along with her two brothers. They fought and screamed the whole time. Achola was holding onto one of her brothers as they took him away. One of the men kicked her and she fell against the wall and she hit her head. That was the last that she could remember; she had blacked out.

Achola awoke to hear her mother crying as one of the men violently raped her. Achola sat up and crawled to the furthest corner in the room. She stayed there, crying and burying her face in her hands. When he was done ravishing her mother, the man began kicking her even though she begged him to stop.

"You thought you were untouchable, eh?" he said, even as he fastened his trousers and continued to kick her.

When her mother could cry no more, she rolled herself into a ball. The man spat on her and gave Achola a sly smile before leaving the hut. He was a young man that they knew from the village. Achola sniffed. She could smell smoke. The hut they were in was on fire! She ran to her mother, lifting her by her arms and dragged her from the hut. All around them the homestead was burning. The granary had already burnt to the ground.

The next morning everyone who had escaped the attacks gathered in an open space in the forest. They were now homeless and very frightened and hungry. Their homes had been burnt down and their domestic animals and poultry had been taken. Whatever they were wearing on their backs was all that they had left. The rebels were everywhere and no one was safe.

Now that they could not farm anymore, they had to depend on the free food that the relief trucks brought them. They did not have the luxury to pick what food they wanted to eat, in what amount or when they wanted to eat it. They tried planting vegetables at the entrance of the camp, but there was only so much that they could plant. For a people who had been used to owning vast pieces of land and large granaries filled with food, this was as good as death itself.

Achola is now 12 years old. Eight years have gone by since the war started. All she can think about now is her little brother and her mother. Her mother gave birth after their father was taken away. When Orach was born, Achola heard the midwife tell her mother, "No matter what, he is still your child."

She said that because Achola's mother would not hold him after he was born.

Right now the rains are falling hard and even the little crop that some people have planted around the camp is rotting underground. The people are starving. The roads have been washed away and now it takes a long while before the trucks get to the camp. They tried to use helicopters to drop food but because most of the ground is covered in water, the food got wet and was spoiled. The trucks of food that were sent out were stuck on the bad roads for days. They could not move forward or backwards. Medical supplies in the camps have run out and the growing number of illnesses is alarming.

Since her mother is too ill, Achola has to go all by herself to get food from the relief trucks. Their hut is at the end of the camp and the food is being served at the other end in an open field. Achola has to move fast now that the news of the trucks is spreading throughout the camp. The other people are also hurrying to get there early so that they can be among the first in line.

Achola holds her containers as firmly as she possibly can and joins the other people along the way. It is a battle that can only be won by the fastest. There are so many people and they are all pushing and trying to run faster than those around them. Some people elbow others or trip them. Anything to have one person less to battle against. In the commotion, Achola is hurt. She falls down twice and hurts her knee.

No one around her pays any attention and they all run past her, some of them jumping over her. Many a child has been known to be trampled to death in such a scuffle as this. Achola stays down for while so that she can compose herself. When she does get up, she cannot run as fast as she was running before. Her mother's words echo in her head: "If you do not bring back food, we will all die of hunger. You must not fail, Achola." Meanwhile, many people have now gathered at the serving point and the trucks have arrived and parked. There are security men keeping the people at bay and ordering them to get into a line before they can be served.

The serving begins and the people at the front can already see that the food is little. In the past they got as much as a sack of beans and a sack of maize as well as a ten litre tin of oil. Now they are lucky if they are given a small bag of rice, a bag of flour, a bag of beans and a small tin of oil. This time there are no tins of oil. There are small two litre bottles, a bag of flour and half a bag of beans. Some people start to complain. This food will not last very long.

Achola finally arrives and she finds that the line is so long that she cannot even see the people serving the food. The sun has now come up and it is quite hot. Some people are seated on their containers because they are too weak to stand.

Agatha is in charge of the food distribution. She walks through the lines, looking at her watch and then at the people in the lines. Then she looks at the food in the trucks and back to the people in the lines. Each time that she looks at her watch, Agatha appears to be impatient, but when she looks at the food remaining and the number of people in the lines, the look of impatience turns to worry. The food will not be enough and the people are too many. There are people who will die of hunger.

Just then, there is commotion at the serving area. There is an old man at the front of the line who refuses to leave even after he has been served his share. He is weak and frail and is asking for more food. The man serving tells him that they cannot give him any more food. The old man pleads, saying that his family is sick and they cannot come and line up. It does not matter what the old man says after that, the serving man will not give him more. The policy is that they can only serve the people in line. His family will have to come for themselves. If they gave everyone their family's share then the food would have already been finished by now. There is so much pushing that the old man starts to get scared and moves away.

There is panic at the back of the line where Achola is. Word is circulating that the food is finished. The crowd starts pushing toward the truck and the security men have to hold them back. Achola is worried; she is thinking about her mother and her brother. The line is getting shorter; there is hope that everyone will get some food even if there is not much left. The beans are finished now and people are getting only flour. Achola is even more worried now; her heart is beating very fast. There are only about twenty people in front of her. Surely she will get something to take home to her mother. At the very least she should get flour that she can use to make porridge.

The serving stops all of a sudden. There is no more food and the people are told to leave and go home. Agatha promises to be back soon with more food. "I will come back as soon as I can," she tells them without even looking at them.

By now Achola has realized what is really happening and she starts to run after the truck. She is crying and mucus is flowing from her nose. The truck slows down and Agatha sees Achola from her window. She gestures to her driver to increase speed. She does not look back except once, when she sees Achola on her knees, searching for any remains on the ground where the men were serving.

Achola is crying hysterically now. She can hardly see the few beans she is picking up. She has no food to take home. She is tired and depressed and afraid of going home. She stops at the swamp and sits. She looks around her, sees nothing but filth. Achola puts her head down. It is throbbing from the hot sun. She falls asleep and awakens when the sun is going down. She has to hurry back home. The government soldiers will be patrolling the camps and they do not like to see people walking about at night. They will not be happy with her and they have been known to lock up people who they think are spies, even if they happen to be little children.

She tries to run, but her knee is throbbing even worse than before. She can only walk with a limp and it is a long while before she actually reaches the camp. Achola hears moaning, it is not uncommon to see people moan in the camps. Somebody dies almost every day. The moaning increases as she approaches her family's hut. She freezes. She drops the empty container and runs inside. People have gathered around and the hut is full. Achola pushes past them.

She takes one look at the bundle of wrapped clothes in the middle of the room and she drops on her knees. Orach has died. Her mother sits motionless next to the body. She looks like she has been crying all day. Two women are supporting her on either side. She looks up and sees Achola and holds out her hands to her. Achola walks straight into her mother's arms and buries her head in her chest. She cannot help but cry.

"I am sorry," Achola manages to say.

"Sshh," her mother says.

"I failed, Mama, I have failed Orach."

This time her mother does not answer. She is numb and she is staring at the bundle beside her. She is so weak that she can barely hold Achola in her arms anymore. The two women want her to rest and they take Achola away from her.

"We will bury him, you need to rest," one of them tells her.

Achola still wants to remain with her mother, but the women will not let her. One of them gestures to another person in the crowd to come and take her away. Her mother lies down slowly. She is too weak to cry, but anyone can see that she is mourning inside.

In the camp, when someone dies, they do not hold long vigils because there is no food to feed everybody. So early the next day, Achola accompanies Orach to his final resting place along with a handful of other people from the camp. The burial ground is near the swamp at the edge of the camp; the place where she always goes to think. Her mother is too weak to go and bury Orach. Achola believes that the death of her brother has made her mother even weaker. Achola lets her tears flow freely as she sees them lower Orach into the small hole which is to be his grave. He has lost so much weight that he looks like a four-year-old child. Achola buries her head in her hands.

The next few days are very slow. The villagers have contributed a small amount of food. Sometimes her mother refuses to eat. She tells Achola that she is not hungry. Achola knows that this is not true. She does not want to let her only remaining child die of hunger. Soon all they have left is porridge. They share one cup a day between the two of them. By now the people in the big city have begun to worry about the people in the camps. It is on the news on every single TV and radio station in the country. Even those people who did not ever care about the war in the North are moved when they see the starving people.

While everyone around her returns to their normal lives, Agatha is never the same again. She cannot get Achola out of her mind. Normally she is able to go to the camp and leave again without feeling a thing. She has never felt attached to anyone or let her emotions get in the way of her work. That day when she drove away from Achola has left her breaking inside. Seeing Achola on her knees scratching for food broke her heart. She knows that there is nothing that she could have done, yet she feels terrible. The whole journey back home she thought about that weeping girl on her bleeding knees.

Achola reminds her of her daughter who is about the same age. Seeing

Achola made her picture her own child begging for food. Agatha is worried that she will not find Achola alive the next time she goes to distribute food. She does not know whether there is still food in the stores to distribute anyway.

There is a rumor going around the camp that the trucks will be back with food. It is almost three days since Achola has eaten the last porridge and she can barely stand up straight. Instead she crawls on all fours just to get around the hut. She sits in a corner and puts her head in her hands. She feels so faint, almost like she is floating on air. Her mother coughs and turns on her side. She is breathing heavily and all Achola can do is stare in her direction. Her mother coughs again and stretches herself out. She breathes her last.

Achola starts to cry. She cannot get rid of the lump in her throat. She is crying but no sound is coming out of her mouth. She starts to crawl slowly toward her mother. Her joints hurt. She cannot see clearly. The room is dark, but she knows that her mother is lying in the middle of the hut. She calls out to her; no answer. It is almost dawn and Achola can hear the sound of the trucks. She thinks she is dreaming. She has now reached her mother and she lies down next to her. She is cold. She slowly closes her eyes and puts her hands around her mother.

The trucks come to a stop and the food is off-loaded. This time there is enough food for everyone. The people are excited; they do not fight to be at the front of the line. They just stand where they can and slowly move forward.

Agatha is amazed. She has never seen them this organised before.

The serving goes on peacefully. Achola is helped to the feeding area by an elderly woman. They walk slowly, Achola almost being dragged along. Achola reaches the truck and falls on her knees. Agatha runs towards her and catches her just as she is about to collapse. Achola takes one look at Agatha and smiles as she tries to talk. She says slowly, "I am on time today…" Then she closes her eyes and lies limp in Agatha's arms.

Achiro Patricia Olwoch hails from Gulu, in Northern Uganda. She has written four books to date and is in the process of self-publishing her first book, A War Song. Achiro bases her writing on real life situations, but adds a twist of imagination to each and every story. She writes because she would like to make a difference in her community through the different stories that she has to tell. Achiro has also written for film and the stage. One of these plays was produced on a radio show in Los Angeles. She presently writes freelance for In Kampala *online magazine and* Inspirit, *the SN Brussels inflight magazine. Most recently, Achiro's was nominated onto the International Women Playwright-Conference's management committee.*

Burning Woman

Michelle Preen

The illuminated words *Prophecy or Potluck* wink at me, indifferent to my pain. A giant wooden wheel spins below them, more words incoherently spiralling and twisting in my mind. When the spinning eventually stops, a phallic arrow points out: *You will rise from the ashes.*

I shiver. Confusion is pulsing through my body, hand in hand with the pain. I am dizzy and nauseous. I have no idea where I am or how I got here. I can smell wood smoke, like when my parents used to take me on holiday to the mountains and we built a log fire in our cabin. I was a girl scout and my dad used to let me make the fire myself.

Far off in the night sky, orange flames leap and curl, leopard's paws slashing wildly at the blackness. I start to lift my head so that I can see better, but my taut neck muscles wrench it back down. I am lying on a blow-up mattress, a lilo of sorts. There is a fleecy turquoise and purple-checked blanket over me. I pull my right hand out from under it where it has been resting on my stomach and a stabbing pain travels down from my shoulder. I wince. Then the wheel is spinning again, churning the words round and round and round. Slowly I start to become aware of the noise too – the throbbing music and the voices shouting and cheering, so many voices all at once. Drums beat out a hypnotic rhythm somewhere far away.

It's as if my senses are being reawakened one by one after a temporary shutdown. I wiggle my toes and realise they are numb. The air is chilly. I see a pair of dusty and well-worn black leather biker boots standing next to the mattress. They look familiar. Before I have a chance to connect with them, a flaming Tyrannosaurus Rex lurches into my line of sight. I scream. My voice is hoarse.

"Someone's awake," I hear through the jumble of voices.

I try to turn towards the voice but my neck won't allow it. I groan.

"Welcome to heaven," says the same voice. Then laughter. More than one person.

I blink a few times and a being appears in front of me. She is wearing a figure-hugging gold bodysuit. There are holes cut in it for her eyes and her breasts. Tassled nipple caps flick around provocatively as she moves. She has no shoes on her dusty feet and her toenails are painted half gold, half black. An ostrich feather headdress flaps around on her head and and as she bends down to stare at me, a little too closely, one of the feathers pokes me in the eye.

"Sorry babe," she says. "Care for a vodka shot? I think you deserve it."

I open the throttle and lean forward as my faithful Yami roars along the dirt road, thrusting up stones and leaving a dust trail for miles behind me. I feel so free, so alone and so alive. This was a good decision – leaving city life and all of its clutter and chaos behind for a few days of detoxing in the wilderness. Just me and my bike and my decision. No television and no cell signal – nothing to distract me, not even a watch. A 'techno famine', my flatmate, Kayla, called it. She cannot possibly contemplate being without her iPhone, laptop and espresso machine for even a few hours, let alone a few days.

We are quite different, Kayla and I. She's the sociable, trendy up-and-coming corporate marketing professional and I'm the independent tomboy with short hair, who seldom wears make-up and works in a sports shop. We've been friends since primary school though, and deep down somewhere we share a common philosophy on life.

I slow down, lift my helmet visor and look around me. It's barren out here in the Karoo. The odd sheep dots the landscape. They forage around eating invisible grass. I imagine they must look like emaciated models under their thick woolly coats.

Kayla has arranged for me to camp for a few days on a farm which belongs to a farmer friend of hers, an ex-boyfriend. I think it must have been the family money which attracted her because it certainly couldn't have been shearing sheep and feeding pigs.

"Are you sure?" she said before contacting him. "This sounds insane."

It took me a day or two to convince her that I was absolutely serious.

"I told him you aren't feeling very sociable right now, that you want some space. He said it wouldn't be a problem, just to give you the directions and no-one will bother you. It's pretty isolated though," she said. "You'll have to take everything with you, including water."

"Just what I need," I'd said.

I stop my bike next to the road and dig in the back pocket of my jeans for the scrap of paper that has on it the directions to the farm. I am not sure if it's my imagination, but my jeans definitely feel tighter. I unfold the note and read the directions. If my calculations are correct, I should reach the farm gate in the next five kilometres or so. A lone crow lands on the barbed wire fence next to the road and looks at me. I am not generally superstitious, but try to remember what one crow symbolises. I seem to think it is unlucky, a sign of foreboding.

I put down my visor and start the bike up again. The crow flies off. I cruise along slowly. The sun is out, but there's a chill in the air. I am really looking forward to this break, but doubt I could live out here. It's so desolate and so harsh.

Within a few minutes, I reach a gate on the left. A sign says: *Rainbow Farm* and under it: *Pieter and Christina Moolman.* I am sure that it has no connection to Rainbow Chickens, but the name brings back memories of driving up to the Drakensberg Mountains with my parents and blocking my nose as we drove past the stinky chicken farms. A wave of nausea hits me. I swallow hard, stop my bike and climb off.

I slip the heavy chain off its hook, pull the gate aside and wheel my bike through. I hook the chain back and stand for a couple of minutes taking some deep breaths. The closer I get to my destination, the closer I get to having to face the reason I came here, and it scares me. I have to make a decision one way or the other. I look down at my stomach. No bump yet, but soon it will be too late.

I ride along the narrow dirt road slowly, respectful of the fact that these people have so kindly offered me a place to camp. Also, I don't want to announce my arrival. About 500 metres along the road I come across a fenced-in patch of old graves. The shiny grey marble glints in the harsh Karoo sunlight. I have always been fascinated by graveyards, but my mother's death is still too recent and it will make me too emotional if I stop and read the headstones. I need to think clearly now, so I continue on the road.

The piece of paper says I should ride until I come to a small dam with a large tree and a windmill. It would be best to camp under the tree, it says. I find it easily. It's a beautiful spot. The ground is hard and dry, but there are a few scrubby bushes. The tree is not large by normal standards but it will provide a little shade. It's nearing late afternoon so I decide to pitch my tent. I undo the stretchies holding it in place on the back of my bike. It's a lightweight one-man tent, perfect for motorcycling. As I struggle to hit the pegs into the hard ground with a rock, the lonely windmill cranks out a metallic tune as it tries in vain to suck up some water from the dry ground. I like the sound.

Then I take the rest of my things out of the panniers. I am glad I decided to bring the down sleeping bag. It's already getting pretty cold. I throw it and my bed roll inside the tent and place my tiny camping kettle and pot next to the tree. For a minute I panic when I can't remember if I brought matches, but then I find them in the box of food between the sardine tins and the Smash. I have always hated the thought of processed and packaged mashed potato, but when space is limited you have to make sacrifices.

Once I am satisfied that everything is unpacked, I wander off into the veld to face my dilemma. How the hell did I get myself into this position? I have been over it so many times in my head and can't believe how stupid and irre-sponsible I was. One crazy drunken night with one of Kayla's clients was all it took.

She had to entertain clients and begged me to come with them to dinner. She made me dress up in one of her short, tight black dresses and she styled my hair and did my make-up. It was obviously successful because the sexy Sean Theron, owner of one of the top restaurants in Cape Town, fancied me. I was so nervous that I knocked back too many Jägermeisters and before I knew it, I was at his penthouse apartment in Camps Bay. I woke up with a staggering hangover and a stunning view of the Atlantic Ocean. I didn't know it then, but I must have also woken up with one of his persistent sperm cells burrowing into one of my eggs. Not surprisingly, I never heard from him again. He doesn't know about the baby and even if I decide to keep it, I'll never tell him.

I reach a little koppie and sit for a while. The land stretches out on either side for miles. A lizard darts across the rock under my legs and I jump. I stare up into the sky. What would my mom have advised? How I wish she was here. I may not have followed her advice, but I would have listened to her wise words and then it would have been easier to make up my own mind. She would have been shocked at first, but she would have supported me no matter what I decided.

I make a small fire that night to boil some water and prepare my supper. Once the fire is out and I'm ready for bed, I sit in the pitch black inside my tent, just listening. I can see nothing and I can almost hear the silence. Then a strange animal sound pierces the stillness and I pull the cowl of my sleeping bag over my head. I hear it again and I fumble around for my head torch so that I can find my taser – the only gadgets I brought with me. I wonder what wild animals live out here. Jackals, I suppose, but hopefully nothing much larger than that. I put the taser in my pocket, lie down and try to get some sleep.

The next day is clear again. My mouth is full of toothpaste when I hear a vehicle coming along the road towards me. I imagine it must be Pieter and really hope that he honours my wish to keep to myself. I am really not in the mood for a polite chat. Then again, the least I can do to thank him for his hospitality is exchange a few polite sentences. I spit the toothpaste into a patch of scrubby bush and take a swig of water from my water bottle, then wipe my mouth on my sleeve.

I see a white bakkie slowing down as it gets nearer. It stops next to the dam and a big unshaven man climbs out. He is wearing faded navy blue rugby shorts and a stained grey T-shirt. Unless he has changed a great deal in the last few years, I can't imagine this is the person Kayla dated. He walks across towards me, spitting into a bush as he passes it.

"So what have we here?" he says in a thick Afrikaans accent. "All the way out in the middle of nowhere."

I instinctively take a few steps back and almost trip over a guy rope.

"Come let me look at you," he says.

I know this is trouble, but I'm not sure what to do. I walk slowly towards my bike, watching his face.

He lurches towards me and grabs one of my wrists in each of his hands. They are huge and hairy and it feels like he could crush my bones if he squeezed a little harder. My heart is pounding. I think about kicking his shins, but he is so strong that I think it will probably just make him angrier.

"Think you're so tough, chicky," he says, "with your leathers and short hair."

He leans in close and kisses my neck. His stubble scratches me and he smells of stale rum.

"Why don't you let me put a baby inside you and make you into a real lady?" he laughs.

Anger and terror surge through me, manifesting themselves in hot, silent tears.

"She cries like a girl," he says.

I am getting panicky now. I still have my taser in my pocket, but he has my hands pinned behind me now and I can't get to it.

"Let's see if you really are one," he says, and he lets go of one of my hands and slides it under my jacket. He gropes around and squeezes my breasts. I vomit on his shoes.

"Stupid bitch," he shouts, and pushes me backwards.

I grab the taser and run towards him, using it to punch him in the stomach. He howls like a dog and falls to the floor writhing.

I have to think fast. I leave him thrashing on the floor, quickly flick off my flip-flops, tug on my boots and zip them up. No time to check for scorpions. My hands are shaking violently as I grab my helmet off the handlebars and jump on my bike. Luckily I left my keys in the ignition, or else goodness knows how long it would take me to find them. I start the ignition and silently thank my bike for being so faithful, and then I race off without looking back. I will retrieve my tent and other belongings later and find somewhere else to stay or maybe even head home.

I drive for about three kilometres, where I find a side road. I travel along it until I find a patch of bushes where I can conceal myself and my bike. God knows what he would do to me if he found me now. I park my bike and climb off. The adrenalin that got me here has ebbed and I crumple to the ground and sob. I can't even phone anyone. When the wrenching sobs subside, I curl up in a ball and lie in the dirt, just staring ahead of me and stroking my stomach.

"It'll be alright," I say over and over. I am not sure whether I am reassuring myself or my unborn child.

About five hours later, when I am feeling weak from hunger and thirst, and pretty certain that the monster will have gone, I drive back to retrieve my stuff. I open the gate cautiously, looking around me constantly and listening for any sound of a vehicle. I find my tent has been slashed with a knife. That beast. Everything else seems okay though and I pack it hastily into the panniers. I decide to take the tent with me because I don't want the Moolmans finding it and launching a search for me. I'll contact them when I get back home and tell them what happened. Or maybe I won't.

I kick some sand hastily over the fire pit I made the night before and lean over to pick up my small camping pot. It is filled with a yellow liquid. I lift it to my nose to smell it, then recoil and toss it away as I realise what it is. The filthy bastard has urinated in it. I cannot bring myself to take it with me, so I kick it under a bush, scan the area once more to check that there is nothing else left behind and head off on my bike back towards the main road.

Once I'm through the gate, emotions overwhelm me – relief, anger, regret, hatred. They all swirl around in my head, colliding with one another and giving me a headache. I crank the throttle as far as it will go, wanting to put as much distance between me and that monster, hoping that the speed will purge the stink of him from my nostrils. All I can think now is: "What if he had harmed my baby?" Then I know I have to keep it.

I am driving too fast, but it feels therapeutic. I feel in control now. I am an experienced rider and there are very few other vehicles on this road. I lean down as I take a corner. The dust billows around me. I take another corner and then everything falls apart. I feel the bike skidding out from under me and my knee hits the gravel. I see a red car coming from the other direction, and the last thing I remember thinking is: "Please protect my baby, please."

I am propped up against a door on the back seat of what looks like an old VW Beetle. I open my eyes, but struggle to focus. I feel drugged. And sore, so terribly sore. Every part of my body either throbs or aches. I look around for blood but can't see any. I touch my stomach. No intense pain there.

"Check that sign," a voice says from the driver's seat. "This road eats tyres for breakfast!"

Then another voice, the passenger, laughs and says: "Lucky for us it's almost supper time."

I close my eyes again and drift off.

When I don't reply, the gold apparition asks again: "A vodka shot for you, darling?"

"No alcohol for me, thanks," I say in my croaky voice.

She looks at me quizzically.

"I am starving though," I say, to divert her attention.

"That's a good sign," she says. "There's loads of food."

She takes my hand and helps me up. I am so stiff.

"How long have I been here?" I ask.

"Not too long."

She leads me to a low table with brightly coloured cushions scattered on the floor around it. We are under a cerise pink Bedouin tent. Spread around the edges, but still underneath it, are small two- and three-person tents. Grace Jones's deep, masculine voice sings "Ring of Fire" on a generator-powered sound system in one corner of the tent. A huge glitter ball hangs from the centre of the tent. I see a hand-painted sign at what must be the entrance that says *Scarem Harem*. A long, narrow Persian carpet leads from the entrance to the table.

"Sit," she says, pushing me down onto a cushion.

The table is covered with an array of delectable food – date balls covered in coconut, koeksisters, chocolate brownies, little quiches, samosas, toffee apples and lots of other scrumptious goodies. A little different from tinned sardines and fake potatoes, I think. Two other people sit at the table. One is dressed as a zebra. I am not sure if it's male or female, and the other is a man. He is naked and painted bright blue all over.

"Where are we?" I ask.

"Told you," says the gold woman. "Heaven."

I am seriously beginning to wonder.

"No seriously," I say.

"AfrikaBurn," says the blue man.

I look blankly at him.

"Burning Man?"

When I still look bemused, he says: "It's an arty party in the desert." He stands as he says this and my natural instinct is to look down at his crotch. My face heats up and turns scarlet when I see the words, *my face is higher up*, painted just below his belly button.

"Well, a bit more than that," says the one in gold. I am relieved to have someone else to focus on.

"It's about radical self-expression, self-reliance, that sort of thing."

She points to the *Prophecy or Potluck* wheel I saw earlier and says: "That's our artwork."

I'll ask more questions later, but right now I need to eat. I have just stuffed the remains of a syrupy koeksister into my mouth when something hits me in the face.

"Here," she says. "This T-shirt is cleaner than what you've got on and a little more funky. Come let me help you."

I look around for somewhere more private to change.

"Oh, don't worry about us," she says, wiggling her breasts.

I look at her nipple caps and laugh. She helps me to get out of my shirt. It's hard to lift my arms, but the more I move, the easier it seems to become. I slip on the shirt she has given me and look down at my chest, at the words emblazoned across it: *A Fierce Desire Burns Within Me.*

"Oh God, I really hope so."

Michelle Preen lives in the coastal village of Kommetjie, Cape Town with her husband and daughter and an assortment of pets. She is a graduate from the University of Kwazulu Natal and currently works in the field of environmental communications and media. Her story, "Whispers from the Wild", was published by Black Letter Media in the anthology The Short Story is Dead. Long Live the Short Story!, as part of Short Story Day Africa 2012. That year she was also placed in the top 20 in the international Writers Weekly 24-hour Short Story Contest. Michelle has had four stories published in YOU, one of South Africa's top-selling English magazines. One of her stories was also selected in 2011 for publication in an anthology of YOU's best short stories over the last ten years. You can follow Michelle on Twitter @mpreen or www.michellepreen.com.

Hyena

Ramonez Ramirez

In the indescribable way that dreams take hold of slumbering prey, the hyena stood in front of Sophie.

Every muscle in its neck contracted in rhythm to the muscles around her bladder loosening. Instinctively she crossed her legs. Her handbag strap slipped over her chapped fingertips, and fell to the floor. A cold breeze exploded through the open carriage doors. The station bell swayed over the deserted platform. Traffic lights gleamed in its corroded sheen.

Sophie didn't take her eyes off the hyena when she bent down to pick up her bag. He leaned forward in anticipation, and, licking his lips, he sneered. His teeth were stained, chipped. An infected cut ran diagonally over his left eye, and the scars over his emaciated cheeks and jaw told Sophie that this one was trouble. She swallowed a dry ball of railway-stale air.

On the platform a piece of tissue whirlwinded over a bench constructed from a wooden railway sleeper. It pirouetted over the backrest, and did a double back flip in the flicker of an overhead fluorescent light. The whirlwind twisted further down the tracks, picking up crisp packets, chocolate wrappers and yesterday's bad news.

The tissue floated down and came to rest on the bench seat. Sophie was able to make out its pink floral patterns before the fluorescent tube finally gave up and flickered off.

If you ever run into a hyena again, Soph, tread lightly, sister. Typical survivors' instincts tell them to do whatever it takes, and trust me, they will—Big Mama's words, so clear in her conscience that Sophie could smell the old woman's sour breath. She almost expected the old woman's thick and liver-spotted fingers to take hold of her forearm. The expectation triggered a series of memories.

Sophie was twelve in 1985 when the drought struck in Gojjam Province for the second time in succession. When the talons of civil war steadied their grip in and around the Northern provinces, the crops failed again. The Ethiopian government's failure to reach out to the famine-stricken areas forced

Sophie and her parents to flee south in the back of a battered army truck driven by her uncle who was a soldier.

"The government's unable to control the situation, brother," Sophie's uncle told her father. "You will have to resettle in the southwest."

"I'm not going." Puffs of dust exploded from Sophie's mother's dreadlocks when she shook her head in protest.

Her husband gave her the look, which meant he didn't want to hear another word about how she felt. Sophie's mother gave him the shoulder for almost two weeks in the back of the truck before the hyenas struck, her last words smothered in dust and black blood as they dragged her by the hair and throat, away into darkness.

Given the state of the roads and the condition of the army truck, it was a journey to forget. Where Sophie now stood in the train, facing another hyena, she could still smell the musty canopy and the stench of rotten flesh; she could hear the soft cries of a dying mother holding her dying baby; she could see the husband squeezing the last drops of mother's milk from his wife's nipple and licking his fingers; she could hear the baby's last breath, a sigh of contentment, deafening over the deflated tyres' dull thumps on the dirt road.

Sophie and Big Mama met on the second last night of their journey. Dehydration had taken its toll on Sophie's mother, and her dreadlocks closed over her wan cheeks when her neck went limp. Sitting opposite her husband (she was still giving him the cold shoulder) she fell forward, her forehead slamming into his thigh.

Sophie panicked and wet herself, only her second pee in twelve days. It burned the red fungal rings which had formed on the insides of her legs.

Big Mama gently took hold of the back of Sophie's soiled T-shirt when the girl leapt up to rush to her mother's aid. Had it not been for Big Mama's steady grip, Sophie would've tripped and fallen over—or even worse—onto the three corpses wrapped in burlap on the floor.

"You're Sophie, right? Hi, I'm Big Mama." The woman's fingers crawled like mopane caterpillars over Sophie's shoulders, thick and soft. Sophie turned to face her. The woman's eyes were the size of shirt buttons, the small, black and shiny type Sophie used to count over and over again on the minister's shirt to keep herself from falling asleep in the village church.

"She's resting, Soph. Sit here with Big Mama and I'll tell you a story."

Sophie shook her head, but her father gave her a reassuring nod.

"Don't you worry, brave one," Big Mama said as she picked her up. "Your mother is going to be fine. I hear they're setting us up near a small lake. We can go swimming there."

"Can't swim." Sophie felt ashamed of herself for acting so cold. The woman was obviously kind-hearted.

"That's alright. You can sit on my tummy while I float on my back. You might think I'll sink, but let me tell you, these babies float like watermelons." Big Mama cupped her breasts and shook them. They jiggled like cows' udders.

A few of the men who were awake sniggered.

"And don't any of you ugly, yellow-eyed bastards think you'll get a piece of the action."

She clicked her tongue and winked at Sophie who had never felt so safe in the arms of a stranger.

"We'll be there in two days' time." Big Mama reached into her bosom and took out a piece of goats cheese, "The smellier, the better. Do you want to hear a story?"

"No. Sleep." Sophie rested her head between the woman's breasts. It was the most comfortable she'd been in weeks. She wanted to thank the big woman, but she couldn't speak. The cheese was delicious. It crumbled over her lips and melted over her tongue, causing a strange sensation like it was swelling up. Sophie would have loved to hear a story, but she wanted nothing more than a good night's sleep.

Hyenas.

Sophie heard their howls as they ran towards the truck, one pack from the east, the other from the west. Big Mama put her hands over Sophie's chest when their vehicle braked and skidded off the road. Rocks and stones scraped the undercarriage, and one of the rear wheels burst. Dust particles and dry grass settled over the canopy like a drizzle when the truck came to a standstill.

Sophie tried to get to her mother, but Big Mama wouldn't let go. "There, there, brave one," Big Mama whispered, "Listen to me." Big Mama was taking deep breaths. "There's nowhere to run. They will smell you out in no time. I need you to lie down between those bodies before the hyenas reach the truck. Right now that is the safest place for you. Either you get in there or they're going to take you."

Sophie's mother started sobbing. Sophie's father and three of the 'yellow-eyed bastards' got up, each armed with a machete.

The hyenas' footsteps were drawing near.

"Get down, you idiots! What are you doing?" Big Mama hissed. "They'll kill you."

"We're not going down without a fight," Sophie's father said. "They want guns and women. If you all look dead, there's a chance. Cover her mouth."

Big Mama put a hand over Sophie's mouth and pulled her closer, her other hand covering the girl's exposed ear.

"I'm so sorry, Sophie," her father whispered. He leaned over and kissed his daughter on the forehead, his lips hot against her skin.

He gave Big Mama *the nod* and made space for Sophie to crawl in between the dead and lie down on her back. A scream of anguish bubbled up in Sophie's throat, but the stench of rotten flesh was too pungent for her to take another breath. And just when she thought things couldn't get any worse, Big Mama lay down on top of her, supporting her weight on the corpses either side of Sophie.

One of Big Mama's nipples poked through a rip in her shirt and touched the tip of Sophie's nose. She turned her head to the side, and although her little hidey hole was dark, and although the corpses had been wrapped in burlap, she was certain she was staring into the glowing eyes of the dead baby in its dead mother's arms. Sophie thought she was dying when she lost all feeling in her legs.

Sophie's father reached for the last few pieces of cloth stashed away underneath the wooden seats and covered Big Mama.

"Don't move a muscle, Sophie," Big Mama whispered.

Sophie could hear the hyenas barking orders for her uncle to get out. The driver's door hinges squealed.

"Don't shoot!" her uncle begged.

Two shots were fired, and her uncle didn't speak again.

Sophie felt the vibrations of her father's footsteps as he moved towards the back of the truck. "On the count of three," he whispered to the yellow-eyed bastards. The truck shook violently when they jumped out the back. The roar of automatic rifles rang out in the sky, and Sophie heard four dull thuds when their bodies hit the ground.

She started to hyperventilate. Afraid that she was going to cry out, Sophie reached for Big Mama's nipple and put it in her mouth.

Sophie heard a groan. She knew it was her mother groaning and bit down hard, sinking her teeth into Big Mama's flesh. Someone stepped onto the back of the truck.

"One of them is still alive, boys," the man shouted. His announcement was met with whistles and hysterical laughter.

"We're going to treat you *real nice.*" There was a struggle and the burlap came off. Sophie was sure she heard her name whispered between her mother's hysterical shrieks and moans. She bit down harder on Big Mama's nipple.

Through a gap between Big Mama's arm and one of the corpses, Sophie saw a giant of a man lifting her mother over his shoulder. Climbing out of the truck, he waved at the rest of the hyenas.

Sophie's mother's screams were muffled by their howls.

The carriage doors still hadn't closed when Sophie's eyes fell upon the oversized black lettering printed on the sign above the doors: WHITES ONLY.

The hyena snarled.

Her bag strap slipped off her shoulder. The half-loaf of white bread at the bottom of the bag sent a soft echo through the empty train carriage as it hit the floor; the pink plastic Tupperware box popped its lid and sloshed chicken broth over her papers.

When the doors hissed shut, Sophie smelled the bitter film of sweat lining her armpits. The hyena's nostrils flared, and Sophie noticed that his dilating pupils were eating away at his irises, blue, like his uniform collar.

The floor felt like rubber when Sophie stepped to her left. The train conductor mirrored her movement.

The train wheels squealed and a puff of steam rose over the grimy carriage windows, momentarily blanking out the outside world.

He sneered again when Sophie stared up in disbelief at the WHITES ONLY sign.

She left her bag on the floor and took a step back. Her dreadlocks clung to the sweat on the back of her T-shirt.

The conductor took a step forward.

He was sinewy – frail almost, and his nails were caked in filth. Sophie knew the look in his eyes; he was starved for violence.

"It's not a fokken staring competition! What do you think you're doing?" The man had a thick Afrikaans accent. Cocking his head to the side, he reached for his baton. "This is a whites only carriage. So, you want to be a whitey?" He rubbed his crotch, "Maybe that's what you want – to ride the white train? It's your lucky day, *you black slut.*"

"Now, pick up your bag and go stand over there," he pointed towards the toilet cubicle. His face was starting to glow with eagerness. The wound over his eye was purple with infection.

Before grabbing her bag, Sophie noticed that almost all of the soup had seeped through the bottom of her bag, forming a piss-yellow puddle on the floor around it. She was staring at her reflection in the oily drops when Big Mama's words found their way into her head again: *A typical survivor's instinct tells them to do whatever it takes, and trust me, they will.*

"Of course," Sophie said under her breath when it dawned on her that she had been one of them all along, one of the survivors. "I'm … I'm a … *hyena.*"

Sophie grabbed her bag, turned and sprinted down the aisle towards the door at the other end of the carriage.

"Hey! Get back here!"

Sophie heard a grunt so loud she was certain the man was about to grab her by her hair. She glanced over her shoulder only to see him slip in the puddle of soup and fall in slow motion: the soles of his polished boots, covered in railway station soot and filth, came up high over his head. The strain on his face was frightening. The open wound over his left eye burst and beads of saliva shot from his mouth. The baton bounced off the floor. His wrist snapped as he landed awkwardly on his right arm, and the back of his head thudded against the floor.

Sophie hit the emergency button.

It took about as long for the train to come to a standstill as it had taken Big Mama to get the army truck started on the night that Sophie's parents were murdered.

They didn't know which direction to take. Having covered a safe enough distance from the rebels, Big Mama stopped the truck.

Sophie and Big Mama slept for a few hours before the stench of the dead bodies in the back of the truck woke them. Big Mama laid them on the ground while Sophie started digging a shallow grave in a sandy patch of earth underneath an acacia tree.

"I'm sorry, Big Mama," Sophie said.

"What on earth for, dear child? None of this is your fault. If there's anyone that should be sorry, it's me. I can't shake the feeling that God is punishing everyone for something my generation has done." Big Mama wiped the tears from her cheeks and then wiped her hands on the back of her dress.

"I'm sorry for biting you. You know, on the –" She pointed at the blood stain over the big woman's left breast.

"Oh, that. Don't be silly. You did the right thing, Soph. It hurt so much that I couldn't make a sound." Big Mama smiled, "Now, let's get out of here. I think it's best if we just keep moving. Do you want to get up on the roof and throw down one of those jerry cans? There should be enough petrol to take us to the border."

"The *border*?"

"If we're lucky, Kenya. I have a relative near Lake Victoria. A chicken farmer. We might be able to stay with him and get some work."

"How are we going to cross the border, Big Mama?"

"We're going to drive across, my dear. God knows, He owes us."

She didn't know why, but it was with trembling hands that Sophie took off her gumboots. Only when she sniffed did she realise that she had been crying. Wiping the tears on her T-shirt sleeves she stepped off the train when the doors opened.

It felt to Sophie as if the cold breeze was slicing open the scars over her bare legs, and the railway gravel felt like broken glass underneath the balls of her feet.

There was a steady build-up of murmuring voices. A few of the other passengers stuck out their necks to see what had happened. Others got off to get a better idea of what was going on.

The pungent smell of the train's steel wheels against its brake-shoes plugged Sophie's nostrils as she crossed the tracks, and she imagined herself with Big Mama in the front of the army truck when its engine ceased on the Southeastern Botswana border.

Things didn't work out for them in Kenya. Big Mama's relative, a scrooge of a man with a bad comb-over and gold-rimmed glasses demanded they pay rent the minute they set foot onto his property. Big Mama pleaded with him, and promised to give him something by the end of the second week of their stay. He refused and threatened to call the authorities if they didn't leave immediately. They left, but not before Big Mama stole the number plates off his truck, six jerry cans of petrol, three chickens and a ten kilogram bag of dried mopane caterpillars.

They travelled from place to place, finding rest nowhere. Eventually, after a grueling three months' journey through the Kalahari Desert, the truck's engine finally ceased in Southeastern Botswana. They didn't know it, but they were standing on the Limpopo River bank on the South African border.

"Well, this is far as she's ever going to go, Sophie. Who would've thought she'd make it this far?" Big Mama coughed because of the stench of the molten rubber fan belt.

Sophie nodded. "Who, indeed."

They constructed a raft sturdy enough to take them across the river. At sunrise they were floating downstream.

Sophie cut through the bush adjacent to the railway line, and after a brisk twenty-minute walk she arrived at Big Mama's shack.

"How was your day, Soph?"

"Not so great, Big Mama. I ran into a hyena."

"They're everywhere these days. I told you not to work so late."

Sophie smiled. "I brought you some bread soaked in what's left of the chicken soup."

"Smells divine, Soph. Thank you."

"It's not exactly what you'd call a feast."

Ramonez Ramirez is a short story author, novelist and poet. He has published articles and short stories for moneyweb.com, and is an active member of the writing sites Periodiccomposition and Gotpoetry. When he's not writing, Ramon teaches English writing skills in the most bombed country on the planet, or farms rice with his wife and three daughters in the north-east of Thailand. You can visit him at www.periodiccomposition.wordpress.com

Fizz Pops

Hamilton Wende

I was eleven and a half when I went to Veld School for the first time. My heroes there were all army guys and Durban surfers. Durban surfers were cool and they said "poison" when they meant nice or good like: "Aaay, the surf's poison today, ek sê."

There were only three or four army guys at the camp. They had just finished their year's training and they had jobs as assistant instructors at the camp. They were eighteen or nineteen years old, but one guy was nearly twenty. The army ous were much cooler than the Durban surfers. They had been on the border. They didn't take shit from anybody.

Most of us were about 11 or 12 years old, except Sylvester. Sylvester was 15. He was the son of an army sergeant from Bethlehem. He wore thick, round glasses and if you looked at him from the side, they made his eyes look huge and swollen like a guppy's and he blinked whenever he didn't understand something.

But Sylvester had ballhairs and chorbs, and he had a real Gillette razor with a silver handle that he used to scrape the pale fluff on his chin with once a week. He was not much taller than me, though.

When he came to Veld School, he had all the real army gear from his old man: T-shirt, "browns", boots (he had big feet), waterbottle, and even a real bayonet with authentic-looking scratches on the brown-painted scabbard.

I remember him on the first day when we were all waiting to be told what to do, walking into the long brick-walled dormitory that we all slept in, his army boots clunking and squealing on the cold concrete floor.

"Howzit, howzit there, howzit man," he said to everyone sitting on their beds, feeling lonely and missing mom, as he made his way down the corridor like some adolescent royalty figure.

"You can call me 'Chickman'," he announced as he swung his army balsak onto the bed next to mine. "I'll teach you anything you need to know about chicks. Just ask, hey." He winked at me. He lay back on his bed, and stared up at the ceiling for a few moments. I didn"t know what to say. I carried on reading my book – *The Hobbit*.

"What's that? A book?"

I looked up to see Sylvester sitting up on one elbow staring at me.

"Ja," I said. "It's really good."

Sylvester blinked, and the skin around his nose wrinkled up and his eyes narrowed behind the thick lenses of his glasses. He turned over and started rustling around in the top of his balsak. He pulled out a copy of *Scope* magazine, fresh from the dusty shelf in the cafe, and opened it to the bikini-clad centrefold.

"Check at this, man," he said, holding the magazine up in front of me. "How are those tits, hey?"

I had never seen the inside of a *Scope* before. The girl was very beautiful, with long blonde hair and a smooth body, but to me she seemed to come from somewhere that must be far, far away. She didn't look like any of the girls I knew, who were mostly skinny and wore black one-piece swimming cozzies from their St. Catherine's uniform and smelt of pool chlorine and wet hair like rat tails. There was something unreal about the way she smiled at you from the smooth, shiny pages of the magazine and about the way she had staples in her tummy.

"Jussis, I love pulling my wire, man!" Sylvester said, holding the magazine up with one hand and scratching his balls with the other. "I dig to lie on my bed and turn off all the lights in my room, then I crank up Albert Hammond's 'Free Electric Band' fullblast and wank in time to the drums."

We learned a lot of things at veld school. Every morning we had lectures. They taught us about drugs and jeans and the real meaning of the peace sign and about how the communists planned to take over South Africa and, after that, the world. They also taught us about pollution and overpopulation, and showed us slides of Japan and Taiwan and other overcrowded countries in the East where you could see people living on sampans in crowded harbours and how the Japanese policemen had to wear masks and take oxygen breaks in little booths when they were directing traffic because the pollution was so bad. From those slides we could see how lucky we were to be South African.

After lectures we had lunch and then we did training. The first day the instructors took us all out to a mealie field and we watched them shoot a tree trunk with an FN rifle. After they had finished up the magazine, we all walked over to the tree and we saw how the bullets had gone all the way through the trunk, just like they would through a terrorist's body.

They also taught us camouflage, and told us how the American GIs in Vietnam lost the war because of 'gorilla' warfare. They told us how the VC would camouflage themselves in the jungle and then ambush the American soldiers. Sylvester put up his hand and told us a story that his dad – the army sergeant – had told him: the VC actually camouflaged themselves on the road. They put tar on their bodies, every-thing. And when the Yanks came in their big trucks and jeeps, the VC just wiped them out.

When we had learned camouflage, we did manoeuvres. The instructors divided us up into two armies: the red and the blue. There was an old abandoned farmhouse that had been standing since the Boer War in the valley below the dormitory build-ing. The blue army had to defend the house, the red army, of course, had to try and infiltrate it. I was in the blue army.

We ran all over the koppies looking for reds, and when we found them we had to stalk them and then jump up and shout: "blam blam" – which was meant to be the noise an FN rifle made, and then we had to tie a piece of blue ribbon around his arm to show that he was dead.

One of the Durban surfers who was in the red army put black shoe polish all over his face and arms and legs and wrapped himself up in a Basotho blanket and put on one of their hats.

He infiltrated the farmhouse, just walked right past all the blue army 'soldiers' waiting in ambush along the road leading up to the house, and past the guards at the gate. He walked up to the army instructor who was our blue army 'commandant', and said, "Middag, baas."

It was only when the guy from Durban took off his hat that the 'commandant' recognized him. He was furious with all of us, and after the manoeuvre was finished, he got the whole blue army together and told us that it was a good lesson for all of us.

"D'you know why he got through?" the instructor asked. "Because why, you don't take the trouble to notice black people and what they are doing. You've got to notice everyone. You've got to learn to identify your enemy."

On Saturday afternoons we had tuckshop. We all had to line up outside the little brick office with a dusty cement floor, a wooden counter, and a python skin and a cowhide Zulu shield with an assegai and knobkerrie on the rough white plaster wall.

We were all allowed to spend 30 cents. The favorite things to buy were green Sparletta Cream Sodas and cherry Fizz Pops with sweet sherbert inside. Sylvester always bought Chappies bubble gum, and he would come up and read us Chappie Chipmunk's 'Did you know?' questions on the inside of the wrapper to see if we knew the answers.

Did you know? 155

Rhinoceros horn is composed of compressed hair.

Did you know? 56

Touching frogs does not give you warts.

Did you know? 900

The blue sky is only the reflection of the sea.

After tuckshop we had free time until supper, and we hung out near the rough stone dining hall with nothing to do, until Sylvester started a telepathy club. He told us that we should learn to practice telepathy so that we could communicate secretly with each other in the mountains when we were going to be fighting the terrorists.

We used to practice until well after dinner, our heads bowed over the bowls of pap and spaghetti sauce in the dining hall, screwing our eyes up tight to help our concentration and thinking of squares and circles and colours …

"I've got it, I've got it, I've got it! It's a square!!!"

"Nearly, nearly! I was thinking of a triangle, which is nearly a square, so we must be getting close."

And then we would bend our heads over again, screw our eyes up into our brains and think until we got little amoebas that floated in front of our eyes, and wouldn't go away.

"Okay, okay, okay, there's it! I've got it this time! It's red, you're thinking of red!"

"Of course, you've got it! I was thinking of a Swiss army knife! Wow, man, this is uuumaaazzzzing!"

"Poison, man, poison."

After tuckshop, the highlight was Sylvester's *Scope*. I didn't tell him that I hadn't ever seen inside one before, but I gave him one of my Fizz Pops and three Chappies from the tuckshop so I could borrow it. I lay on my bed trying to look at it all cool and natural, like I had seen hundreds of pin-up pictures before.

But the girl was so beautiful. She was posing on a beach and her long, straight blonde hair fell halfway down her back.

She was 19 years old, and was wearing a blue bikini. Her eyes were brown and filled with laughter, and her name was Sandy. It was written there on the bottom of the page in her own curly handwriting – XXX Sandy.

I fell in love with Sandy. I never told anyone, but my heart ached for her. I would imagine the two of us walking on the beach, holding hands – maybe in Durban, with the surfers staring enviously at us. The sun setting over the ocean. The two of us kissing and laughing and telling secrets together, and me knowing that her smile and the smell and touch of her soft golden hair would fill my life for ever and ever.

Veld school was good. It was teaching us to be men. I remember one day sitting around after tuckshop…Did you know? 199 Glass manufacture began in Egypt… two or three of the army ous came over to speak to us. We all sat there in a circle, listening to their stories. I remember Sylvester sitting on the ground with his thick round glasses and his real army bayonet strapped to his waist.

The army guys started telling us about girls:

"I'm telling you ous, you are all still piepie-jollers now, but when you learn about chicks, your life will be completely different from what it is now."

"They are lekker things, but you"ll never understand them."

"Aaaay, I chaff you, the best thing is to be sitting watching rugby with your cherry there to keep you warm."

Oh, Sandy, Sandy, Sandy... would we understand each other? And would you be my cherry?

The mountains: Swartkop, Groenkop, Steenberg – the foothills of the Maluti range – stretched up into the blue sky behind us. The wind coming off the slopes rustled the leaves of the gum trees, and the clear morning air was filled with the faint smell of eucalyptus, and of dust and dry winter grass.

And we all sat, transfixed, listening to these older boys, our heroes, telling us about serving up on the border. The Caprivi strip, Angola, Rhodesia… those names echoed in all of our hearts. That's where they had been, fighting terrorists in the bush. That's where the action was. And we weren't going to make the same mistakes that the Americans made in Vietnam. No way. We weren't soft from sweets and Coke and Fanta and drugs like the Yanks. We knew camouflage, and how to identify our enemy...

"'The funniest thing, though, is catching a terr, and finding ways to make him talk. You tune him: 'Hey, join us, and we won't kill you.' So he reckons: 'No, sweet, that's what I'll do.' So he joins you and you tell him he can be a parabat. So you take him up to two, three thousand feet in a plane with a couple of 'bats, and they jump out with their parachutes on. And then you tell him: 'It's your turn to jump now,' and he says: 'But where's my parachute?' and you just start laughing and point at the 'bats floating down to the ground. 'They're doing it for real, but you don't need a parachute – you're just practicing.'"

Just practicing. Hell, they thought it was funny! Imagine that: just practicing. Everybody was laughing. Sylvester most of all, he was leaning back holding his side and slapping his free hand on the dusty ground. Those army ous were tough, hey? The way they just looked at you when they told that story – so cool, and serious, like real grown-up men. But they were also scary, and even though I laughed at the story with the other boys it made me feel scared.

All that afternoon I wanted to be alone. I wanted to be alone and think of Sandy, and of how it would be one day when I was grown up and of how I would be taller than Sylvester and have a girlfriend like Sandy, and of how I would have stories of my own to tell her and how I wouldn't have to give Sylvester a Fizz Pop to see her in her bikini.

Hamilton Wende is a freelance writer and television producer based in Johannesburg. He is a regular contributor to From Our Own Correspondent on Radio 4 on the BBC. He is a columnist for The Star in Johannesburg and his articles have appeared in many international and South African newspapers and magazines. Journey Into Darkness, a documentary on the genocide in Rwanda he worked on for the BBC with producer David Harrison and correspondent Fergal Keane won the 1994 Royal Television Society's International Current Affairs Award. A Life Less Fortunate, a film on children in South African prisons he worked on with Belinda Hawkins of SBS won the 1999 United Nations Association of Australia Media Award.

ACKNOWLEDGEMENTS

A good writer possesses not only his own spirit but also the spirit of his friends.
– Friedrich Nietzsche

Every publication is the result of a team effort, and none more so than this. Special thanks to Karen Jennings whose keen eyes and dedication added shine and polish to these stories. Nick Mulgrew of Paperight for the cover and page design, as well as his encouragement, enthusiasm and support. Arthur Attwell and the Paperight team for their support and for Nick Mulgrew's book design skills. Candace di Talamo for the cover illustration. Colleen Higgs for her support and publishing advice. The team at Worldreader for their support, encouragement, cash and endless offers of extra help should we need it.

Special thanks to the *Feast, Famine and Potluck* competition judges: Consuelo Roland, Isabella Morris, Novuyo Rosa-Tshuma, and Petina Gappah; and the readers: Alé Steyn, Aoife Lennon-Ritchie, Casey B Dolan, Diane Awerbuck, Henrietta Rose-Innes, Lindsay van Rensburg, Sheryl Kavin, Tiah Beautement and Rachel Zadok.

Also to the judges of the *Fairy Tales, Myths and Legends* competition: Byron Loker, Cat Hellisen, Damaria Senne, Helen Brain, S.A. Partridge and Verushka Louw.

And every writer who entered the competition, whether they made it into this anthology or not.

The prizes for the competitions were donated by All About Writing, Andie Miller, BooksLive, Botsotso, The Caine Prize for African Writing, The Lennon-Ritchie Agency, Louis Greenberg, Helen Moffett & Paige Nick & Sarah Lotz in the guise of Helena S. Paige, Modjaji Books, Rachel Zadok and NB Publishers.

Without the sponsorship, financially and in kind, of the following organisations and individuals our scope would have been much smaller:

ALÉ STEYN • ALL ABOUT WRITING • AOIFE LENNON-RITCHIE • BEATRICE LAMWAKA
BOOKSLIVE • BOTSOTSO • BRANDON CARLLAW • BYRON LOKER
THE CAINE PRIZE FOR AFRICAN WRITING • CASEY B DOLAN • CAT HELLISEN
CHARLES BUKOWSKI • CINDY DE BRUYN • CRISTY ZINN • CONSUELO ROLAND
DAMARIA SENNE • DIANE AWERBUCK • FREDERICK J. CARLETON
FOX AND RAVEN PUBLISHING • GLEN MEHN • HELEN BRAIN
HEART & SOUL PHOTOGRAPHY • HENRIETTA ROSE-INNES • HELEN MOFFETT
ISLA HADDOW-FLOOD • ISABELLA MORRIS • JOANNE MACGREGOR • JEFF MCLUCAS
JOE VAZ • JULIAN BRACKER • KARINA MAGDALENA SZCZUREK-BRINK • KATIE REID
THE KITCHIES • LINDSAY VAN RENSBURG • LITNET • LOUIS GREENBERG
MACK LUNDY • MICHELLE PREEN • MODJAJI BOOKS • NB PUBLISHERS
NA'EEMAH MASOET • NICK MULGREW • NOVUYO ROSA-TSHUMA • PAIGE NICK
PAPERIGHT • PETINA GAPPAH • RAHLA XENOPOULOS • RICHARD DU NOOY
S.A. PARTRIDGE • SARAH CASSIN • SARAH LOTZ • SEAN FRASER • SHERYL KAVIN
SOMETHING WICKED • SUSIE DINNEEN • TIAH BEAUTEMENT • VERUSHKA LOUW
WORLDREADER

And to all the writers and readers of African fiction, we thank you.

Rachel Zadok and Tiah Beautement
The Short Story Day Africa team